A Life Lit by Sunlight

A Selection of Letters written by Philip Erskine while serving with the Scots Guards 1953 – 1971.

Edited and compiled by Murray Naylor, Summer 2020.

First published in Great Britain in 2020 by Quacks Books

Copyright © Murray Naylor

isbn 978-1-912728-25-1

All rights reserved by the copyright owner. The moral right of the author has been asserted, British Library cataloging in publication data A Life lit by Sunlight, A Selection of Letters written by Philip Erskine while serving with the Scots Guards 1953 – 1971.

Set in twelve point Baskerville, justified with occasional text italicising with three point leading, headings centred in Baskerville bold, running heads centred in ten point. Page size 170mm x 245mm with a gutter margin of 15mm, head 25mm, for-edge 25mm and foot of 25mm, illustrated with photographs and maps printed litho on a one hundred gsm chosen for its sustainability.

The Editor wishes to acknowledge the considerable help he has been given in compiling these letters in one volume. In particular to Michael Sessions and Katy Midgley of Quacks in York and to Alex Swanston who drew the maps. He is also indebted to those who have supplied photographs.

Published and printed by
Quacks Books
7 Grape Lane
Petergate
York Yo1 7hu
info@quacks.info
www.radiusonline.info
0044 (0)1904 635967

Philip when ADC to the Governor General in Wellington 1960

Contents

Foreword	vii
Editorial	ix
Philip Erskine's Obituary	xi
Section A. An Ensign in Egypt	1
Section B. ADC to the Governor General of New Zealand	51
Section C. The Royal Guard, Balmoral	111
Epilogue	129

Foreword

After leaving Charterhouse Philip yearned to go to Art College and to paint in Paris like his idol, Toulouse Lautrec. His father, General Bobby, supported this idea until Granny revealed rumours of Lautrec's sordid lifestyle. That same evening Philip's father penned a letter to the Colonel of the Scots Guards. Father's fate was sealed. He served in the regiment for twenty 'gloriously happy' years. It was during this time that he married my mother, Fiona. They soon started a family with three small children. Father ended this period of his life with more friends than anyone I have ever met.

Those who knew Father will attest to his charm, his wit, and his insatiable sense of humour. Ida's Valley was a virtual thoroughfare of visitors from Princes, Dukes and Archbishops to ordinary and humble folk. Father and Mother entertained on an unparalleled scale for over forty years.

Father's gastronomic escapades eventually took their toll on his health to which end he was forced to attend the local gym in Stellenbosch. He did this most reluctantly dressed in a pair of tracksuit trousers, his finest London leather shoes, a striped shirt made by his Saville Row tailor and of course his regimental tie.

Father had tremendous wisdom and fortitude, which contributed to the smooth running of his family and every other area of his life over which he had an influence. He had so many diverse interests. He adored talking about everything under the sun. He loved to share his political opinions and cherished the ensuing debate. He had strong views on Current Affairs, about Church Affairs and Church History, about Antiques and Art, and Porcelain and Furniture, about The Boer War or any other war, and about long forgotten Kings and Queens. He loved reading. He literally devoured books, and as a result he knew an awful lot about nearly everything,

It was his painting which dominated the last 20 years of his life, and it will be his paintings that will live on as his most enduring legacy. His canvasses were large abstract landscapes, inspired by the Impressionists, bursting with the beauty and the vivid light of the Cape.

Father also wrote a great deal throughout his life, and never more so than when his health prevented him from venturing outdoors. His letters were circulated far and wide and were enjoyed by his many friends and equally large family. His letters from Ida's Valley provide fascinating observations of the all aspects of life at the Cape spanning a period of over 40 years from the darkest days of Apartheid to the modern era.

In this compilation Murray Naylor has taken immense trouble to edit Father's letters written whilst serving in the Scots Guards. Our family is deeply appreciative of this commitment to an old friendship. These letters provide a most refreshing perspective on events and about an era now almost forgotten.

Edward Erskine.
Natal, South Africa.
June 2020.

Editorial

Philip Erskine served in the Scots Guards from 1953 to 1971. His life and his achievements as a soldier were well set down in his obituary published in the *Guards Magazine* following his death in South Africa in 2013, a copy of which is printed on the following pages. Philip was a very talented man: he was fun, generous, possessed of a sharp intellect and was very engaging. Above all he loved his contact with people. Soldiering was always an ambition and he exulted in regimental life and the company of his brother guardsmen. Painting was equally a passion and, as readers of his letters will discover, during his time in New Zealand in particular he developed his artistic skills with great success. In short, he was a man many admired, few disliked and who, wherever he went, spread light and joy to those he met. His family's choice of the title for this book of letters is therefore entirely appropriate. Never probably destined to be an outstanding soldier himself, he brought warmth and kindness to his relationships with those with whom he served. His father was a most successful and highly decorated wartime soldier and, by all accounts, Philip idolized him.

So why this collection of letters? Philip had a gift of being able to tell a story. For instance, once retired from the Army and living at Stellenbosch in the Western Cape, he wrote regularly to his siblings recording in detail but with a light touch, what was happening in his adopted land. Those letters also found their way to many friends. However, they are not the purpose of this compilation since they are specific to South Africa; if, one day, somebody can find the commitment to consolidate them in a single volume, I suspect they could be a sensation.

Rather, the letters in this book record some of those written by Philip to his family during his military service between 1953 and 1971. They emanated from his pen in one of three places where he served as a soldier, all of them widely different. His letters from the Canal Zone in 1954 depict a newly arrived young officer, commanding a platoon on active service. They describe the life of a close-knit battalion with an important role, but yet able to relax and enjoy itself when the opportunity arose. Many of those who read these letters will be able to identify with Philip's descriptions. The letters also highlight some of the tensions which arose as Britain's imperial responsibilities began to reduce after World War Two.

His year as an ADC to the Governor General of New Zealand involved a totally different setting. Life in a country far removed from Britain, the emphasis almost exclusively on the world of diplomacy and government, and the chance to discover an almost idyllic landscape, and to indulge his joy of painting, all intrigued Philip. He clearly enjoyed life to the full but manifestly didn't take himself or his role too seriously!

Finally, two months in 1967 commanding the Queen's Guard at Balmoral brought a contrasting set of challenges and pleasures, graphically described by Philip. In his commentary Philip's acuity of observation, his ability to smooth bruised relationships and his sense of humour are never far below the surface. The success of the Guard under his leadership as noted by The Queen's Private Secretary at the end of the tour, says it all.

The task I set myself was to edit Philip's letters so that they might be read more widely. This first meant gaining agreement from Fiona, Philip's wife, and his family to the publication of the letters in a single volume. This permission secured, the letters needed to be edited in order to eliminate duplication and to remove anything of a sensitive nature. There was also a need to modify certain passages but to avoid doing so in a way that altered the essential characteristics of Philip's original writing. If this at times results in a slightly disjointed approach, so be it. Thereafter some maps to help those possibly unfamiliar with the places involved, and a few illustrations have been added.

I feel privileged to have been allowed to undertake this task by Fiona, and Eddy Erskine, with the support of the wider family. I hope the outcome will be to their satisfaction and will give them pleasure as well as reinforcing their pride in Philip's considerable achievements. I hope the same will apply to his many friends elsewhere and in particular those who knew him in the Scots Guards, the regiment he was always so proud to serve.

Major P.N. Erskine

Late Scots Guards

The events of Philip Erskine's early life cannot be told without telling his family story, since the two ran in parallel throughout his childhood and ultimately influenced his entire life in 'The Shadow of his Father' whom he adored.

Philip was born in August 1933. His father was General Sir George Erskine GCB KBE DSO, who survived the horrors of the trenches and stayed on in the Army to become a career soldier. His mother Ruby was the eldest daughter of Sir Evelyn de la Rue. His early childhood days were interrupted by a looming crisis in Europe, and at the age of six he watched his father go off to war, his regiment, The 60th Rifles, suffering a severe mauling at Calais.

Philip's prep school years were spent on the move. He attended St Augustine's in Eastbourne and then Cheam in Tidworth for just two terms. Such was the unsettled nature of a wartime education that he and his brother, Robert, were shuffled from one school to another. Finally, the two boys settled at Lindsey's School – 'Sherborne Prep' – in the Spring Term of 1941, where he remained until June 1947.

Philip and Robert shared a remarkable wartime childhood, and with it developed a warm bond of friendship that endured. They lived a country life far from the city bombings, raising livestock and tending a kitchen garden. Their mother taught them to cook and bake and sew, and they took part in all the farm activities. They made hay in summer, fed the pigs and milked the cows. They were encouraged to paint, to work hard, and to appreciate nature. Wartime life was tough but simple and Philip loved those happy days with his brother and his favourite companion, his pony *Joey*.

Boarding school was less appealing, a cold and uncompromising environment. Philip, as the son of a famous general, was expected to behave accordingly, the only privilege was the occasional call-up to the headmaster's office to hear news of the war and his father's division. He longed for the holidays.

Philip's public schooling took place at Charterhouse, where he went in the autumn of 1947. Here his love of painting grew during his teenage years. He studied under Ian Fleming Williams, a truly inspirational tutor, and it came as no surprise to anyone when he won the major art prize in his final year. By now the family had been extended by the late arrival of his sister Polly, whom he absolutely adored. Polly was the inspiration and the 'Principal Addressee' of the polygraph letters that spanned over forty years of his life in South Africa.

During the post war years Philip's father held a wide array of commands, this time accompanied by his family. The simple country style holidays gave way to grand tours of Berlin, Egypt and Hong Kong, where father was Commander-in-Chief. The shorter holidays were spent in the Scottish Borders with his uncle, Sir Eric, happy and fun-filled days spent shooting, rabbit netting and all manner of country pursuits. In Philip's recollections from this time: 'I spent one of my holidays in Berlin. We were the first British family to go to Berlin after the war. One of the events I shall never forget was a visit to Hitler's Bunker. At one of the Four Power meetings the Russians announced they were going to demolish Hitler's Chancellery and Bunker. Father asked if he could see it before they demolished it. As a result, a small party of us were shown round…..I don't think many other people saw the bunker, as it had been boarded up. Nothing had been moved, all the furniture was in place, there was no ventilation, papers were strewn everywhere, there were several inches of water and oil on the floor and the air was horrid.'

When at last the childhood days were over he had to choose a career. He would have liked to pursue his love of painting but, with the dismal prospects for artists in the years after the war, he followed his father into the Army. Three months at the Brigade Squad were followed by Sandhurst, and he was commissioned into the Scots Guards in September 1953. He attended the Platoon Commander's Course at Hythe and Warminster, and from there joined the 1st Battalion in Egypt, where he served in Port Said doing guards and cable patrols, followed by six months in a tented camp, near Moscar.

The Coronation was the next great event in which both he and his father took part. A few days later his father was called to Churchill's office and sent to East Africa as Commander-in-Chief, during the Kenya Emergency. Philip visited his father in Nairobi during this time. He then went on to Pirbright to train National Service recruits, and at the end of 1955 was sent out as the Signals

Officer to the 2nd Battalion in Germany. In November 1956 the Battalion returned to Chelsea Barracks and spent the following year doing Public Duties in London.

In October 1957 Philip was appointed Adjutant of the 1st Battalion and spent a year doing Public Duties, including Windsor and the Queen's Birthday Parade. In November he moved with the battalion to Germany. Nearly two years later he was appointed as ADC to Lord Cobham, Governor General of New Zealand. While there, he had time to paint, but sadly in the process he developed lead poisoning, which he ingested from his paints. The illness had long term consequences. Lead poisoning has the feature of returning and over the next few years he suffered several attacks. On his way home from New Zealand he spent three months at the Cape and married his first cousin, Fiona Radcliffe. This was to be the most marvellous, successful, and happy marriage, and happy union that lasted for over 50 glorious years. It was a marriage that was admired by so many people.

In January 1961, he was posted to Wellington Barracks, commanding G Company of the 2nd Battalion. A year later he went to Regimental Headquarters where for a short time he acted as Recruiting Officer. Next he was appointed as Equerry to HRH Prince Henry, Duke of Gloucester. Between 1963 and 1965 he returned to the Regiment as a company commander, taking part in the funeral of Sir Winston Churchill in January 1965. In May 1965 he was posted to Headquarters Aldershot District as G3 Ops, Intelligence and Security. In July 1967 he spent two months as Captain of the Queen's Guard at Balmoral Castle. During this time The Queen Mother asked him to paint a mural at Corndavon Lodge which she much delighted in. His father had been a favourite at the Court of King George VI and Philip continued his friendship with the present Queen.

Tribute by Andrew Parsons:

> *'The Scottish Division were not wildly amused when we did the Ballater Guard for the first time in 1976. Philip was not only an inspired choice but very much the right man in the right place at the time. He knew everyone at Balmoral and with his wonderful sense of humour (under pinned with a sharp intellect) he was able to defuse any moments of tension. He made it all fun for everyone with his familiar*

giggle at the amusing moments of which there were many. For example, when the ponyman blindly followed the path he followed everyday straight through the Royal picnic. It was a wonderful year for weather and grouse. The guardsmen rarely if ever got wet on the hill. Records were broken in the Guard Gamebook and the 1967 totals will never be surpassed. Philip was a very good shot. There was a strong Sergeants' Mess and much participation in local events – including Ant Forbes doing well in the Ballater Hill Race and entertaining Princess Anne playing 'Puppet on a String' on his pipes.'

Philip's battalion moved to Chelsea Barracks in 1968. Here he commanded Headquarter Company and again spent the summer doing public duties and, although he had passed the necessary entrance exams, was unable to proceed to the Staff College on grounds of poor health. Philip left the Army and so began the third phase of his life – '42 more glorious years in South Africa'. He arrived with his family aboard the RMS *Windsor Castle* in January 1971. After spending several months in Somerset West searching for a new home, he found and quickly purchased a beautiful Cape Dutch homestead *Ida's Valley*. For the next five years he poured all his energy into the restoration of the house, creating a most remarkable family home and one of the finest homesteads in the Cape. He and Fiona entertained there on an unparalleled scale, with many thousands of visitors, ranging from Royalty and Heads of State to the most humble of folk, and almost all held spellbound by his wit, wisdom and radiant charm.

With the restoration of *Ida's Valley* substantially complete, Philip turned his creative attention to the Church and the world of culture. For ten years until 1985 he immersed himself in fund raising for the Church. He sold Christmas cards and from the proceeds founded the St Mary's Trust. He served as churchwarden, attended Synod, and was appointed to serve on the Archbishop's Executive. He also became chairman of the Antique Collectors Society of South Africa, founded the Cape Cultural Press, and published a magazine *Antiques in South Africa*.

Philip was asked to serve on the South African Military History Museum and on the Board of the Michaelis Collection in Cape Town, and also served on the Stellenbosch Museum Board. He co-founded the Historical House Owners Association, serving as Chairman for eight years. During his time he succeeded in having, not only *Ida's Valley Homestead*, but the entire valley declared a National Monument, and subsequently a National Heritage site. He served on two committees of the National Monuments Council, and was on the committee of the Van der Stell Society, for which service he was awarded a gold medal for his work in conservation. He also served as President of the Guards Association of Southern Africa for 23 years.

By 1985, he turned back to his painting, attending an Art School in Cape Town on a part time basis. From 1987 onwards he devoted most of his time to painting. Over the next 18 years he had 14 exhibitions. He derived enormous pleasure from his painting and his wonderful works were highly sought after and sold in the grandest galleries in Johannesburg. His art will remain his most enduring legacy.

Although he suffered from a wide variety of health problems throughout his later years he never let them dominate him, nor deter his indomitable spirit. He died peacefully in Stellenbosch on 23rd July 2013. He is survived by his devoted wife Fiona, three children, Rupert, Lucy and Edward, and a large pack of adoring dogs! 'A life lit by Sunlight'.

Obituary published in *The Guards Magazine* in 2013 and reproduced with the Editor's permission. The author of the obituary has not been identified.

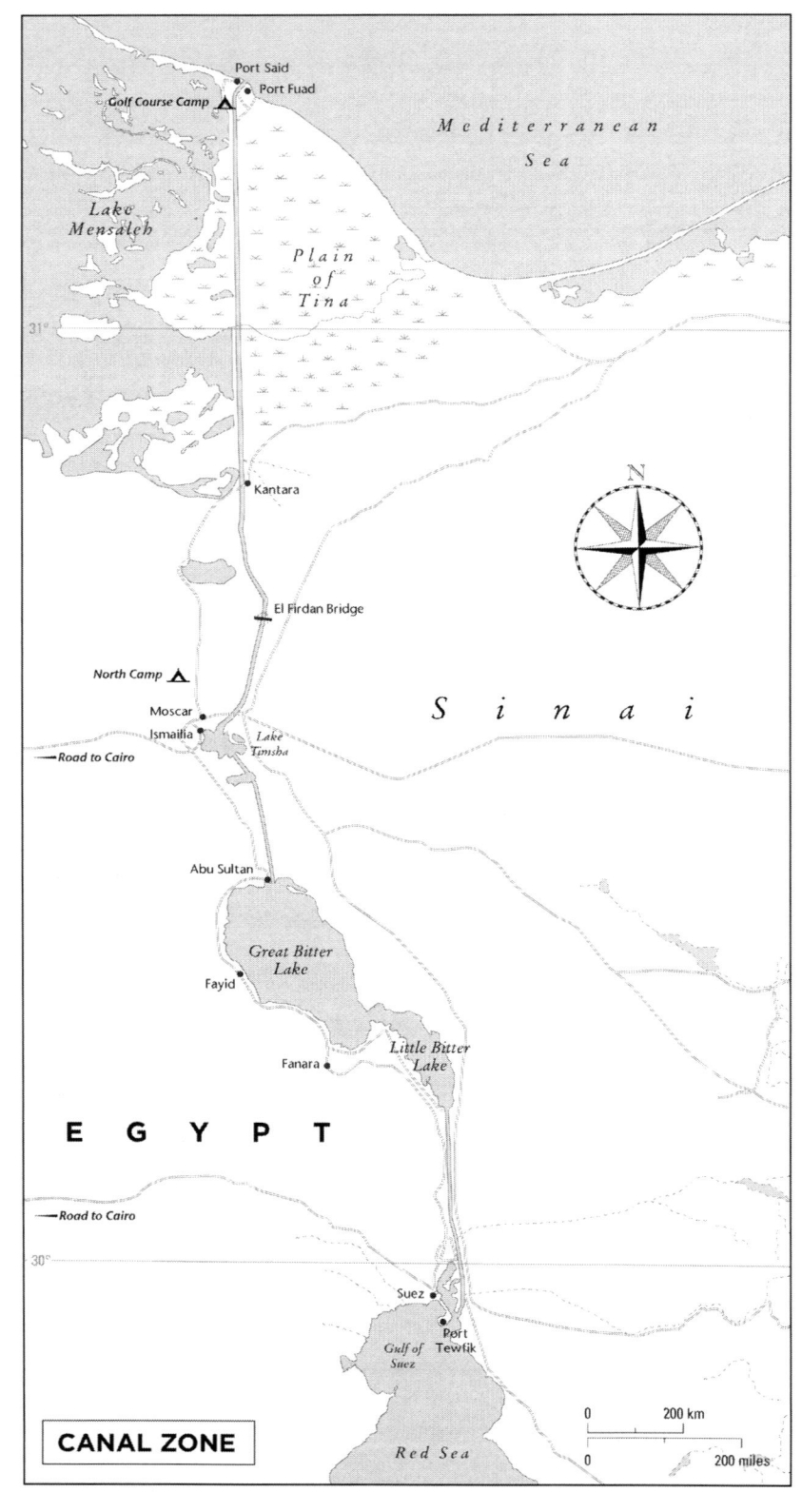

Section A

An Ensign In Egypt

Letters from Philip Erskine to his parents while serving in the 1st Battalion Scots Guards, January to December 1954.

Between 1952 and 1954 the 1st Battalion undertook a tour of duty in the Canal Zone. Operations during much of this period involved security duties guarding military installations, or properties used by the Suez Canal Company to allow uninterrupted transit of the waterway by international traffic. At one time around 170 soldiers could be deployed each night, although this total was later reduced to a more manageable level. Troops serving in the Zone moved between camps situated along the length of the canal and were under command of British Troops Egypt (BTE).

Politically Egypt was in much turmoil during these years. King Farouk abdicated in 1954. He was replaced by General Neguib who was later overthrown by Colonel Nasser. Thereafter the latter ruled for many years becoming a pivotal political figure in the Middle East. Later following the signing of a treaty between Britain and Egypt all British troops were to be withdrawn from the Zone, the last leaving in June 1956.

Colonel Peter Fane Gladwin was commanding the battalion for most of this time. Philip Erskine arrived in the Canal Zone in January 1954 to take command of a platoon in Left Flank. He already knew the area well since his father had earlier commanded BTE from 1949 to 1952 and the Erskine family had lived in the Zone. By 1954 Philip's father, General Sir George Erskine, was in command of British troops in Kenya engaged in fighting the Mau Mau uprising in the colony. Meanwhile Philip's mother had remained in Britain.

Philip's letters have been reproduced with minimal editing although some have been deleted where they duplicate news already given.

11th January 1954

Cheriton House Templecombe, Somerset

I have been meaning to write to you for days. I hope the New Year has started off on a positive note. You may well ask why am I still here? I was supposed to report to Pirbright on 2nd January and take a draft out to the battalion. I was told not to report till 8th so last Friday I had everything packed in tin cases, I said good bye to everybody and duly went off to Pirbright. I went along to the Scots Guards Company office, there was nobody about except one ensign who told me that the draft I was taking had been postponed till 19th January. It seemed they didn't want me just hanging around, so I was told to go home and they would telephone me when I was wanted. It's all rather frustrating – but that's life so I am back at home again.

I am trying to sell my motor bicycle, it's not going very well, I have hammered the hell out of it for 18 months. I think I shall be lucky to get £40 from the garage; I may get more if I advertise in the Western Gazette.

25th January 1954

1st Bn Scots Guards, Port Said.

I arrived here on Friday evening. I had a pleasant journey. I got to Googe Street, the London Assembly Centre, on Tuesday at midday and was told I was not wanted till the following morning, so I thought I would go down to Rusper and see Granny and Diana. I haven't seen them for ages and this was a perfect opportunity. I had tea and dinner with them, then the last train back to London. I slept the night in the shelter and was surprised it was as good as it was. Next morning we were taken to Stansgate by bus and were airborne by 11.30. It transpired that we had the contract manager of Skyways with us and the crew were out to impress him and it was laid on thick... free drinks all round - 'ad nauseam'; as a result there were certain passengers worse for wear by the time we got to Malta.

We were only two hours in Malta, otherwise I would have gone and seen Rosemary Annette. Then we flew on to Fayid, a long boring flight and arrived there at 2 am. Ghastly time to arrive. We were taken to a transit camp in Fayid but as the battalion was expecting a draft, which meant sending down two trucks, I just had to wait there for 24 hours. And as you can imagine it was an anti-climax hanging round there for a day in a very dreary spot. However, that night there was quite a party. Some armed Egyptians got into the NAFFI and were disturbed by the sentry and at 3 in the morning there was a hell of a shoot out ... one dead and one wounded. Everybody heard the drama except me who slept through it all!

I was fascinated driving up from Fayid along the route and past many of the places I knew so well. When I arrived the Colonel said 'I think you know the cook'. Who do you think I found here? Cookie, our old cook. I said you and mother sent your best wishes, I think he was thrilled to see me. Everybody agreed the cooking was first class; he is obviously doing a good job and is much appreciated.

I start work seriously tomorrow, the Adjutant, Neil Ramsay, has arranged a short introductory course to give one an insight of the workings of the battalion. I sit behind the Adjutant at Commanding Officer's Orders for two weeks or so. Meanwhile I have been posted to Left Flank, commanded by John Ramsay. He has only got two other ensigns, (Donald Marr and James Ogilvy.) You know better than I do the sort of routine we have, a mass of guards to mount every night, escort duties and cable patrols, but I think the internal security position in Port Said is more relaxed than down south. There is almost no time for training; indeed there is almost nobody to train. We live on the guard roster. I have got a tent to myself at the moment; it is very bare, one bed, one cupboard, one table and one chair. I expect I can improve on it bit by bit.

I hear we are moving to North Camp at Moscar in April and we are due to leave here next February. It was originally November; its a pity as it means we will be here for Christmas.

There is very little else to tell you, except to say I am delighted at last to be with the Battalion. It has been a long time, (three years and three months,) since that day in October 1951 when you bid me farewell at Waterloo Station on my way to Caterham and the Guards Depot. I hope I can get down to see you in Kenya . . .

27th January 1954

Golf Course Camp MELF 27

Thank you so much for your letter. I have now been here a week and I am just beginning to know my way around - what happens in all the tents and huts. I am on a young officers course with Anthony Hopkinson, (his uncle is the Under Secretary of State at the Colonial Office,) you may come across him. He is a National Service officer and arrived two days ago, we are doing the same programme and lectures on the various duties of characters such a Sergeant in waiting, the Piquet Sergeant. We attend Guard Mounting in the evening. *(The wonderful words of command given by the piquet officer.... "Stand still the Inland Water Transport Guard, remainder right turn, to your duties quick march. " I have never forgotten those words.)* The other night we went round with the piquet officer visiting all the guards at 3am. The Quartermaster, *(Donald Fraser,)* gave an excellent talk about what his department does and how they function. We attend both Adjutant's and Commanding Officer's Orders, we sit behind and listen to the business being conducted. The course lasts ten days. In between times I go along to Left Flank Company office where John Ramsay gives me the odd job to do.

As you know the secret of this sort of life is to create an atmosphere of acute activity, the enemy is boredom. There is something going on the whole time. Last week was the inter company novice boxing, then that followed by various boxing matches. Last Saturday we fought and won against HMS Gambia, we beat the Beds and Herts, we fight the Welshmen next week. We like to think we have a formidable reputation! Last Thursday, in contrast was the Battalion concert - a highly amusing evening. Every company did a turn and the guardsmen loved it. There is an amazing amount of talent in the Battalion. On top of all this, there is a football knock out competition this week in the afternoons and next week a hockey league knock out. You might suspect we are doing nothing but sport but in fact we are providing over 120 men a night for guard duty. We work hard and play hard and morale is sky high. I know it is pure swank but everybody says we are the best Battalion in the Canal Zone.

The story outside the camp is less happy. There have been quite a number of incidents. We don't hear a great deal, and there is a lot of gossip flying round, those going down to Moscar pick up much of it. They bring back news, what other battalions have been doing, it's second hand and not very accurate. We think the acts of terrorism are being orchestrated from Cairo, who blow hot and cold on an almost daily basis. We have to be on our toes and alert the whole time and I am sure it makes a huge difference when our guardsmen are seen by the locals as smart and alert, they are far less inclined to take a chance. A sloppy appearance is asking for trouble. There appear to be tensions in Port Said at the moment, only a few of the shops will serve us. Last week Simon Artz refused to serve some officers. The Second in Command, (Michael Fitzalan Howard) was turned out of the main hotel at the weekend. Hardly any guardsmen 'walk out' in Port Said, which is just as well as they would be vulnerable. But it changes every week, one imagines on orders from Cairo.

4th February 1954

Golf Course Camp Port Said

Quite a lot of things have happened since I last wrote. I finished my introductory course yesterday and the trouble began in earnest. Let me explain. A decree came down from the Orderly Room that every platoon commander was to give a lecture to his platoon on venereal disease, as there had been several cases in the battalion, which is considered unacceptable. Frankly, what I know on the subject is almost the square root of zero! I have a platoon that consists mainly of hardened Glaswegians, who know a thousand times more than I do. I struck on the idea of getting my platoon sergeant, Sergeant Simpson 09. He was brilliant, in broad Glaswegian he gave a vivid description, a lot of grunting of what happens to those who suffer, telling them their noses will drop off, and they will lose their ears. The guardsmen's eyes were all dropping out; he made the point better than I could have done.

John Ramsay and Donald Mar went off to Fayid yesterday leaving James Ogilvy and myself to amuse the company for two days. The afternoons were easy as there was a battalion football match, and in the evening, education, but the mornings were the problem. We agreed that James would look after the first half until 10.30 and I would take them on the 30-yard range, firing the Sten [gun] till midday. Half way through the shoot the Commanding Officer turned up... but he seemed impressed and my activity went along smoothly.

As you may know, anyone wanting to go into Port Said has to go in groups of four and I have been in several times - to make up numbers. After what we had heard last week, earlier in the week the shopkeepers all seemed very friendly, shaking hands and producing cups of coffee. Then yesterday, they did their best to get us out of their shops and there was a very different atmosphere - almost hostile. We had great difficulty buying anything. We think it must be official; the word comes down from Cairo.

There have been a few incidents during the week. Three nights ago the NAAFI warehouse was burnt in the middle of the night, it was a very impressive blaze and a huge amount of stores were burnt, including a lot of rubber articles, which caused a very unpleasant smell across our camp. The warehouse is just outside the camp; we don't find guards on that building. It is rumoured that the manager fired it himself as he was selling to the locals and thought he was being caught. There have also been several cable-cutting incidents. They might have been acting as a decoy for other trouble, the culprits were never caught.

We had a company smoker on Wednesday night. The guardsmen loved it; we started by having a formal dinner in the cookhouse then there were turns by individuals, you can imagine - funny stories getting dirtier and dirtier, others getting up to sing with beer flowing. To my horror I was detailed to get up and sing... "We want the new officers to sing us a song." James jumped to his feet and sang about ten verses of Eskimo Nel. I was nimble enough to realise it was the Padre's birthday and got them to sing him 'Happy birthday' and I got away without further activity!

The programme in the next few weeks looks quite daunting, a Brigade exercise next week and followed by Spring Drills and endless inspections.

13th February 1954

I love your letters and news. I have just got back from spending 4 days with the Irish Guards at Fanara, helping to run the ranges for the BTE Rifle Meeting. It wasn't much fun spending all the time in the butts, but staying with the Micks was great fun. We played roulette every evening, over a whole week I came out about even. I knew several Micks, Martin Carlton Smith was my term at Sandhurst and had just arrived, we had been on the same courses at Warminster and Hythe. Richard Cheney, Welsh Guards, was also helping with the rifle meeting. I think you knew his parents.

At dawn tomorrow we start an exercise. We drive down to south of Suez and spend most of next week in the Red Sea Hills. I understand we take up and create a strong defensive position and then do a withdrawal across the hills at night. I am expecting it will be quite demanding.

You would be amused to hear when I drove down to the Micks at Fanara I went down the Canal Road through Ismalia. The town was looking exactly the same and I could even spot the exact place where I had painted the mosque but they had cut all the branches off the flamboyant trees. I suppose it was to clear the cover preventing snipers shooting at our vehicles - even Fly Town hadn't changed. It is hard to believe there has been a lot of trouble and shooting as it all looked as it always did, except for a few roadblocks.

The big joke this week is the story about our Regimental Sergeant Major. I should explain that Bob Thomson is a huge man, impressive in every way. He lives in a flat in Port Fuad. He was woken in the night by a burglar, he grabbed the wretched creature and hurled him out of the third floor window. I believe every bone in his body was broken but he managed to limp off like a hard hit rabbit. We rather think he and his friends won't came back for more!

Oh, I must tell you - the big operation today was the battalion being photographed. Every company and every platoon, in every order of dress, every sporting team was also included. The photographer was your old friend Sarkis! He was just about to photograph us when I went up to him and introduced myself. I said I was so pleased to see him looking so well, whereupon he poured out all his troubles. He kept saying, "Ah zi General was so wonderful. Ah zi Lady made my life. Ah zi Polly she was so good looking". He stopped his activity and just wanted to go on talking. "You must tell zi General ... you must tell zi Lady" and so on! It was a somewhat embarrassing scene with nearly a hundred men waiting and in a hurry to get on. All this happened in the middle of the square. But I assured him you had the highest regard for him. I think this made his day.

Don't fuss about me. I am very happy and it's wonderful to be with the Battalion. There is a very good spirit in the Battalion and I don't think it is just idle swank, but we have earned the respect both of the Army and the locals.

28th February 1954

Thank you for your letters. I am vastly interested in all you are doing in Kenya.

You will be interested to hear, we had a break from all our guard duties, which is always welcome, and got back yesterday from a brigade exercise, Exercise Chatterbox. Apart from ourselves, the Welsh Guards, the Beds and Herts and the usual hangers on at Brigade Headquarters took part. Colonel Peter got us to the concentration area 24 hours early as he wanted to practice moving across the desert as a whole battalion. I think it was to give everybody a chance of making a bog up before the main exercise started, also to give everyone blisters. Both aims were achieved!

I know you know that part of the world well. We left this camp on Sunday afternoon arriving at the Concentration Area, which was about 25 miles south of Fanara on the Treaty Road. Then on Monday afternoon everybody else assembled and that evening we motored in the dark, lights off to an Assembly Area down in the Red Sea Hills. It was a nightmare of a drive, sixty miles without lights, and made worse by the fact we were the last unit, getting the

dust of 400 vehicles. (They had the RASC recovery out in force).
My 3tonner broke down five miles out from the Assembly Area, and all the RASC driver said "Its been under observation". There were clouds of smoke belching out of the back and it fairly quickly packed up. Another 3 tonner appeared but was little better and that came to a grinding halt after about two miles and we got a tow. The night was made even more unpleasant as it started to rain. The RASC vehicles were a disgrace and everybody had experiences similar to mine, and if this exercise has demonstrated anything it is that something needs doing about the RASC transport.

We spent a rather miserable day hanging round in the Assembly area, waiting for the stragglers to catch up. Then in the late afternoon we marched 12 miles to take up a defensive position in the hills. By the time we got to our destination it was dark but there was a full moon and it was remarkably light under the wonderful clear sky. We tried to dig down as far as possible but it was solid rock, we ended up building sangers out of boulders.

My platoon was far from being anything like the School of Infantry pattern. I had two sections, one with a lance sergeant, lance corporal and four men, the other a lance sergeant and five men also a platoon headquarters consisting of my platoon sergeant, my soldier servant who acted as runner, a guardsman with a rocket launcher and another with a 2 inch mortar, in all 16 men!

Wednesday and Thursday was spent in this position improving our sangers and camouflaging them. The enemy, the South Lancashires and a squadron of Life Guards, were patrolling against us and we had the odd air attack but it was very quiet. General Frankie Festing came and inspected my platoon position. He talked to me for several minutes about everything, the house and garden and asked after yourself. He said he would like your job! I said how much he had liked yours! He says he wants to fly down to see you.

To digress for a moment. It was somewhat farcical, we knew what the enemy was doing the whole time. A sergeant in the Intelligence Corps was sent down to the Life Guards Mess, as a public relations officer with the task of writing a press publication and told to take photographs. Great pains had been taken to make the subterfuge realistic. His land rover had special signs painted on it. The individual was a real smoothie, and had all the patter and in the process extricated all the exercise plans we needed. When he left he told them to send his mess bill to Public Relations, B.T.E. He flew home the following day and was demobilised. The Life Guards were furious and completely hoodwinked!

Thursday evening we did a withdrawal. We were the Advance Guard; our route took us through a narrow wadi, code named Happy Valley. We were expecting to be ambushed and have to fight our way through but never once did we get a whiff of the enemy. We heard later the enemy set up an ambush in another wadi, which the Welsh Guards used, and all hell popped with them... It was rather an anti climax as we had such an easy withdrawal; the exercise ended at 10.30 in the evening instead of dawn on Friday. There was a wash up conference on the exercise by General Frankie at El Balah. We got a fair amount of praise for our effort but the poor South Lancashires came in for considerable criticism and were told they were in an awful muddle from start to finish.

Tomorrow early I go to El Balah and stay with the Beds and Herts to help classify the battalion on the ranges. I imagine I will be there about a week. I hope I can extend my stay down there as long as I can as Spring Drills start next week, which is something to be avoided. The agony lasts two weeks. Everybody gets sharpened up and chased round the square by the Drill Sergeants on three drill parades a morning.

There was only one incident while we were away of any note. In our absence the Ordnance Depot found their own guards for their Base Vehicle Depot (BVD) and the Marines did the cable patrols. One night the cable was cut and the Marine patrol found an Egyptian lorry just outside the BVD looking very suspicious. On inspection they discovered a large amount of tyres, wheels and spare parts of every kind. The driver said he had been told to stay there and then go down to the docks just nearby. The Marine patrol went down to the docks and found a barge half full of spare parts from previous trips that night. The amusing part of the story is that about a month ago the Ordnance Colonel was missing some stores and accused us - our Guardsmen of nicking his stores. Now it has been proved that his own people were doing it and our guardroom is full of their staff including an Ordnance sergeant!

There are wild rumours flying round that 32nd Guards Brigade are going to be sent down to Kenya. Michael Webb says he was tipped off and announced it in the Mess yesterday. I doubt if you can say if it's true. It would be a tremendous boost, as all our National Service men would sign on and you couldn't get a better battalion! The press is full of what you are doing, our papers arrive four days late. Anyway I am longing to come down and see you ...

4th March 1954

Port Said

I arrived back here early this morning from El Balah. I was glad to be back. The ranges were hell and the camp was uncomfortable in the extreme. There was no respite from the wind and the sand gets into everything.

There seems to be little or no repercussions to the Neguib/Nasser revolution last week in Port Said; as a precaution the town was put out of bounds last weekend. It was reported there were a few excited people wandering around in the streets but nothing else. We are still doing the cable patrols, they come round about once a week but so far I haven't had any excitements.

I went into Simon Artz this evening and bought a carpet for my tent for £5, it will make my tent more comfortable. I share my tent now with Anthony Hopkinson who arrived a couple of weeks ago.

I missed the first week of Spring Drills, which are now in full swing, and this week my company are going down to guard the El Fidan Bridge, which will be a pleasant change; the rest of the battalion is acting as enemy for another exercise for the South Lancashire Regiment. Running round in the Red Sea Hills again.

8th March 1954

Port Said

I have not written for several days and only a brief one now. We have been very busy with Spring Drills. Three parades in the morning and the rest of the day are devoted to a tremendous effort to tidy up the battalion area in camp. Everything is painted, the doors, window frames, and fire buckets. The walls are all being distempered, and hours are spent making the company stores immaculate. We have got painting mania! Even the tent pegs get painted light blue, (that is our company colour.) One guardsman even painted the guy ropes of his tent... as the old adage goes "Polish it, paint it, or salute it." In the cold light of day I think we are going potty, but in the circumstances of isolation in the desert where we have got nothing else to do right now, we tend to get an exaggerated sense of priorities.

When I got back to Golf Course Camp I was on cable patrol duty, (it comes round once a week) and I had a mild excitement. I have done these patrols several times recently but so far nothing has happened. It consists of driving up and down the Treaty Road, for about 20 miles south of Port Said to a spot called Kantara, in a quarter ton vehicle, backwards and forwards all night from dusk to dawn. Coming up in the opposite direction is another patrol from El Balah, sometimes from the Welsh Guards, the Beds and Herts or the Royal Marines. On this occasion the cable was cut just beyond my beat near El Balah. I stopped every vehicle on the road and held them up for hours, being as difficult as I could be. I made all the occupants get out and I thoroughly searched each vehicle. Several lorries were heaped high with vegetables. I made them open some of their sacks in the middle of the road. I had nothing else to do, but they were all in a great hurry to catch the morning market. A wonderful situation to be in, time was no object to me! In point of fact the chance of catching a car with cable in it was almost nil as there were several villages on the way where they would have unloaded it. They knew we patrolled the Treaty Road and the Canal Road 100 yards immediately adjacent, we didn't patrol. We feel if we make a fuss and are thoroughly difficult it will discourage cable cutting.

There has been no trouble in our area since I have been here. James Ogilvy had a similar experience the other day when the cable was cut in the Welsh Guards beat and made several vehicles unload everything on the road including a sweet lorry. It took the Egyptian drivers several hours to reload their trucks and I gather there were civil complaints. The Egyptian authorities were told quite firmly, "We had every right to stop and search every vehicle if our cables had been cut, and if you don't like the inconvenience you should restrain the characters doing the cable cutting."

24th March 1954

Thank you very much for your news. I am wondering when it would be suitable for me to come down and stay? I am off tomorrow for ten days with Left Flank; it's our turn to do guard duty at the El Fidan Bridge. Our programme looks very full till at least mid June, and that's a long way ahead.

I wish I knew what was happening in this country. There has been an outburst of acts of terrorism in the last few days, which is obviously backed from Cairo, and it appears to be well organised. It seems to be turned on, then off, and on again. They say the Government is in a very wobbly state and a great deal of subversive pamphlets are in circulation from a whole range of organisations: Ikwan, Communists, Moslem Brotherhood and even Royalists.

Last Saturday when we went into Port Said we were followed round and as we went into shops, a police officer told the shopkeepers not to sell to us. Oddly enough, complaints reached the Governor of Port Said. (They are terrified we will put the town out of bounds to British ships as they pass through the Canal, and that trade is the lifeblood of the town.) We gathered that the police officer was sent back to Cairo! The gossip in the Mess is that we can expect more terrorism - on and off spasmodically, the only trouble is that the increase of incidents means more restrictions and our guard duties increase. It's a miracle that Port Said remains in bounds. The government, we are told could fall any time but nobody seems to know what sort of government will take its place.

Last Sunday evening I was detailed to go to a party on HMS Peacock for drinks and buffet supper followed by a film show. They were a weird collections of officers. I found myself talking to one midshipman and asked his name. I was told he was called 'Peanuts', 'Why?' I asked. "Oh, his father was, a socialist minister called Strachey who was in charge of the 'groundnut scheme in Africa!" I wonder if you ever met him?
 I went on a cable cutting patrol on Monday, nothing happened, there has been very little excitement up our end. A quartermaster was shot near El Balah at the weekend, I don't know the details, and we gather there is a lot of tension down there. John Ramsay decided to get rid of our Company

Sergeant Major; he was an extraordinary man who started life in the RAF Regiment. He was a very good athlete, but carbolic in the extreme. His successor is my old squad instructor at the Depot, Sergeant Ferguson. He's not a bad chap, now it's my turn to give him hell!

28th March 1954

El Fidan Bridge

I have been down here four days. I should explain the El Fidan position has two bridges over the canal. There is the old one, which you will remember, is still in use and is surrounded by a detachment of the Egyptian Army. The new bridge is two miles south and is nearly complete and we are in a position on the West bank on a small hill over looking the new bridge and a considerable length of the canal in both directions. The reason for the new bridge is that the old one needs replacing as it has become unsafe. You will remember how Father controlled the old bridge when there was trouble, a couple of years ago and held a trump card as half the Egyptian Army was over in Sinai. As the tension decreased, we, (the British Army), abandoned the position on the old bridge. I think last August, when there was renewed tension, the Egyptian Army quickly occupied our old position. General Frankie, knowing that the new bridge would be in use within a year put a company in position on the new bridge ... so here we are!

The snag about this camp is that nobody at BTE will say if this camp is permanent or not, as a result they are very cagey about spending a single penny. There are several well-constructed strong points; otherwise we all live in small temporary tents. We have made the Officers Mess tent comfortable with several carpets we brought down from Port Said. We do feel rather out of touch with the news as we don't get the papers but it is extremely pleasant being down here for a short time away from the pressures of battalion life, and the guardsmen are happy with wonderful swimming in the canal. We have great fun when any British Royal Naval ship passes up or down the canal. We dip our flag and Macdonald, our company piper, plays 'Will ye no come home again'. 'Scotland the Brave'. In fact he goes on playing till the ship has passed out of sight! The Navy return our compliments. Then there are exchanges across the water between the guardsmen and the sailors, which are less polite!

Yesterday a Swedish liner passed, which caused great excitement. MacDonald played every tune he knew. All those lovely blonde Swedish girls waved and waved; the guardsmen roared themselves hoarse....I doubt if any of it was understood.

You will be amused to hear I spent yesterday morning in Moscar. It's a strange feeling going back to a place we knew so well. It was all exactly the same; almost nothing has changed except the AKC which has moved into a new very swish building behind the swimming pool. I booked some tickets for BTE Boxing finals next week.

We have heard on the news, there is a real shambles in Cairo, tension is acute and an open split between Neguib and Nasser. We are speculating on the outcome, but what seems almost certain is that renewed tension in Cairo means trouble down here. If I was a betting man - and I am not, I would put my money on Nasser, he is a younger man and seems to have the army on his side. Anyway, all will be revealed soon!

MELF 26 5th April 1954

Port Said

I arrived back from El Fidan yesterday. /We thoroughly enjoyed ourselves, the weather was perfect except for the last few days when it rained and hailed and we suffered a 'Khamsim', one of those dreadful sand storms they have here.

It was a strange existence at El Fidan. The Egyptians and ourselves have our guns pointing at each other. We have a permanent roadblock on the Canal Road, we make a point of being very polite to the Egyptian officers and our sentries salute their senior officer and in return they salute ours. We do some modest training in the morning, John Ramsay, our company commander, lectures us on the finer points of military life. Each of us subalterns finds some modest military activity to keep the interest of the guardsmen, then in the afternoon we laze around swimming and playing basketball. Life appears to have no care in the world, then suddenly there is an incident in the neighbourhood and we are on full alert. But outwardly we are all smiles with our neighbours but our guns are zeroed on them - nicely!

While I was away there was a tragic incident, Guardsman Wallace was shot. He was the Padre's soldier servant and was acting as escort on Easter Sunday. He was shot on his way to collect the padre. I don't know the details. They are very conflicting. The Egyptian Governor of Port Said and his chief of police were extremely helpful and polite to Colonel Peter - certainly outwardly, but the driver of the vehicle told our intelligence staff there was a police officer in the stolen car which they drove to Dammetta with the bandits, where they were stopped and then returned to the police station. The police did nothing, not even attempted to arrest them. The driver of the car had been wounded in the neck but not seriously, he had been held down on the back seat and couldn't remember anything. We deduce the killing was political. It is a reminder that we are on active service and we have to be vigilant all the time.

Life goes on much the same. Last Thursday the whole company went down to El Balah to spend 36 hours in the desert; we fired all our weapons, including 3.5 rocket launchers, mortars and doing some field firing, using live rounds. We had a company smoker in the evening. We made a huge fire and sat round singing songs and drinking beer. I was most impressed by the company talent. I sang a rather feeble rendering of the Rajah of Astrakhan! I am not grumbling but the officer duties in the battalion at the moment are quite heavy. C Company is doing the El Fidan bridge commitment, they took over from us, and several National Service ensigns have gone home. We are doing three duties a week and we are lucky if we get a proper night's sleep more than twice a week.

2nd May 1954

Port Said

I am sorry I have not written for sometime. I will try and bring you up to date. I have been quite busy running a map reading course, also I have been made the battalion swimming officer. I have been told to organise a water polo league. I need two barges to be moored out from the beach to hold the goal posts. I think the RASC with their water transport will help me. I am busy most evenings supervising 2nd class education. The Commanding Officer asked me to give two lectures about Kenya. I think the lectures went down quite well, now several guardsmen want to join the Kenya Police much to the irritation of John Ramsay, my company commander, who doesn't want to lose some of his best men.

We seem to have had a series of amusing parties. There was a travelling theatre group called 'London Laughs'; they consisted of 3 glamour girls who sing, a female comedienne, two male comedians and a roller-skater who did a clever act. The guardsmen enjoyed it and behaved badly making obscene remarks at the wrong moment. You can just imagine 200 sex-starved soldiers watching a tit-show! They all came back to the Mess afterwards and someone got hold of the padre's organ and we had an impromptu performance. We were the chorus; it was lighthearted entertainment and very amusing.

At the weekend we had a very amusing evening. We invited several Grenadier and Irish Guards officers - there were twelve of them - up from the south. We had a splendid buffet supper and played roulette, I had a share of the bank, which we syndicated among five of us and apart from being a very enjoyable evening, I made a couple of pounds.

12th May 1954

I am piquet officer and I have got a few minutes so a quick letter. There was a mild flap and a series of incidents have taken place over the last few days. It had been relatively quiet since the last bout of trouble at Easter.

Some military police were shot up yesterday afternoon and in the evening they captured Captain Wise, after he had parked his car outside Simon Artz. He was blindfolded and eventually released. He is the Police liaison officer, the last person they should mess about with unless it was done by a group who want to embarrass the local authorities.

22nd May 1954

Port Said

We have just had our final inspection by the Lieutenant Colonel, Colonel Claude Dunbar. Part of the programme for his visit was to watch Right Flank do a demonstration of a company attack. Last Thursday I went down to El Balah with Right Flank and David Scott - Barrett, their Company Commander. The object was to help them do a demonstration to show off our skills. Thursday, it was stinking hot - well over a hundred, not a speck of shade anywhere. Then in the afternoon the Khamsim blew, we groped around in a dust storm, we tried to have a practice but it was impossible to make much headway so we retired to the Bengal Club. We started again next morning very early; the temperature had dropped and the dust storm had abated and the demonstration went off like clockwork. Everybody was delighted.

We have had exceptionally hot weather in Port Said. It's not just the heat but also the high humidity, which is the killer. A group of us had rather fun last night, we went to the Casino Palace Hotel where we had heard there was a party in progress. There were masses of French, Greeks and indeed shades of colour of every kind sitting round tables placed round the dance floor, outside in a courtyard. Very glittery, with millions of coloured lights hanging from the palm trees and a strong smell of cheap Egyptian scent. You can imagine the exotic scene.

The civilian population has been very shy of being seen talking to us and indeed having any contact with the Army at all - be they Greek, French, Egyptian or any of the locals, even the British civilians don't want to know us. However, on this occasion I was determined to dance. Over the other side of the dance floor I spied a very pretty girl, incidentally I had no idea of her nationality. All my mates said it wouldn't work and bet I would fail. I walked over to her and with all the courage I could muster asked her to dance. Nothing happened... she didn't move; I repeated my request boldly and politely in French. Still nothing happened. For the third time I cleared my throat. "Mon ami," a long pause, "voulez vous... " It worked, she got up and we launched ourselves onto the dance floor. I had no idea how to do the South American rumba. I stumbled and staggered round the dance floor, I trod on her toes, she nearly fell over, I am sure she was vastly embarrassed and no doubt badly wounded by the experience... Her party thought it hilariously funny but I won my bet. I was proud as punch! Patrick Cobold and the other members of the party tried their luck - but failed. They were all turned down flat!

We got back after midnight, I did a quick change into uniform and as Piquet Officer visited the camp sentries and all the other guards we provide in the Port Said area. When I got to the Ordnance Supply Depot, our sergeant of the guard was all smiles - grinning from ear to ear. He said. "We've just caught an Egyptian breaking into this camp." He was sent back to the battalion guardroom. It is a great achievement to catch a thief; the camp covers a huge area and our guards have to patrol miles of perimeter fencing, which is in poor condition, the visibility is very bad. The Depot is one hell of a muddle; they have piled their stores out in the open, millions of jerry cans and rusting equipment of every kind, giving plenty of cover for a thief to operate. I don't suppose the Ordnance people know what they've got. This character was caught pinching jerry cans and got tangled up in the wire, trying to escape. I went to see him in our Guardroom; he was under the supervision of the Battalion Police Sergeant, Sergeant Marchant. He put him in the next cell where he keeps 'Butch'. He is a very fierce hound, half ridgeback, half mastiff, and the very sight or sound of this animal is enough to terrify the indigenous. He will be handed over to the Egyptian Police tomorrow, no doubt released and back on the job again. One just hopes he is sufficiently frightened by his experience not to do it again while we are here.

Ramadan is keeping everybody quiet. I have been into Port Said several times last week and the place is deserted, not a soul seemed to move, even the ever present gully gully men and the hawkers who hang round the street cafes have gone to ground. There are no shoeshine boys, no flower sellers; only the odd sleepy policeman looking like grim death, lolling against buildings. Ramadan lasts for another twelve days, then I cannot help thinking that trouble will start again, but for the moment everything is dead. My plans for going down to Kenya and see Father are well advanced.

23rd May 1954

Thank you for several letters. There seems to be a very good post between here and Kenya. I think I mentioned in an earlier letter about Owen Varney. (He is a subaltern in the battalion and was at Charterhouse with me.) He asked if it would be possible to get down to Kenya and I wondered if there would be a spare seat on your plane not being occupied by anyone else? If it's difficult - I will tell him and that's that, but I know he would be very grateful if it could be arranged. He knows Dick Cornell as he was at Sandhurst with his brother, John. The other point James Ogilvy wants to know if he can use Egyptian money in Kenya and can he cash an English cheque...

Derby Day 2nd June 1954

Golf Course Camp, Port Said

What a way to spend Derby Day. We heard the race commentary over the BBC World Service. We created quite an atmosphere in the Mess, the fizz of champagne, and cigar smoke wafting around the Mess like the members' enclosure. Trevor Dawson organised a sweepstake. We all drew for a horse, I drew a dud called Moonlight Express, and it didn't do anything. There was a lot of side betting, buying and selling to those who drew favoured runners. Nobody was interested in mine. Ashworth, the senior mess waiter won the jackpot of £63.

After this lighthearted break, the emphasis is on the Birthday Parade on Saturday. The battalion is providing two Guards. I am going down tomorrow to watch the rehearsal and for a briefing; I have been given the task to usher in the V.I.P. stand. I cannot help smiling, as there are a whole series of rows floating round. The number one fuss was over your old friend Stevenson, the British Ambassador. He was asked to take the salute, as he represents the Queen, but he refused and said he would send a representative in his place. The parade is in honour of the Queen's Birthday and some creepy crawly figure from the Embassy was not acceptable. He was told firmly the invitation was to him personally. As you will remember Fayid is littered with generals and senior officers in what we used to call 'Red Flannel Ally" There is some pretty unattractive jockeying for grand seats, and some are being very pushy. "Why does Mrs Deakin sit next to Lady Festing when Mrs so and so whose husband is a Major General gets palmed off with a humble seat in the background?". The Queen's Birthday Parade is a private Household Brigade affair; anyone from outside is welcome as guests and not part of the show. I suppose it's quite normal, the senior wives are intensely jealous of each other. They haven't got enough to do so they squabble over anything.

Oddly enough, the thing that is giving me some problems is doing a painting of Colonel Peter's garden. He insists that I finish the painting before I go on leave. The problem is that it is a non-subject. A few months ago it was blown up by several young officers after a dinner night. It's difficult to get much inspiration out of a few petunias, the odd geranium, a spiky little cassrina tree and a lot of dead grass. However, I have made a start, my imagination has been stretched to the limit.

The hot weather has set in, but it is much worse the further south one goes.

12th June 1954

Golf Course Camp, Port Said.

This week has been very full, the big event has been the Trooping. A huge effort has been put into it. It is very rare for two Guards Brigade - 32nd and 1st - to be serving in one station. The general verdict was that the parade was a great success. There were 4000 spectators in the stands and that doesn't count the number of troops standing round the parade in enclosures. The form of the parade was exactly the same as the one performed on the Horse Guards. The mass bands came from other regiments serving here, the Green Howards, the Highland Light Infantry, the Durham Light Infantry and the Corps of Drums from four battalions of Foot Guards, and pipers from the Micks and ourselves. All the mounted officers were on greys. The Army Commander, General Frankie and the two brigade commanders were on shining black chargers. It was very impressive.

It is the extraordinary feature about serving here. One minute we are on high alert for trouble and indeed we are told we are on active service, and then we stage a most impressive parade that consumes the attention of two whole brigades and the guardsmen indulge in ceremonial duties of a peacetime nature. I wonder what message it sends to the Egyptians?

After the parade Lady Festing asked me to play tennis and swim. When I got to the house there was a big conference in progress, which was soon over, they all came out onto the veranda to talk, including your friend Ian Hamilton. General Frankie was apparently very ill, he had dosed himself up to take the parade and then went straight back to bed. There were two other officers there playing tennis, David Greenacre and James Malcolm from the Welsh Guards and Tim Riley from the Micks (General F's ADC.)

The other event of the week has been having Ivie Benson and her all girls band here. They drove up here on Friday morning and gave the battalion a performance in the afternoon and then had tea with us. There were seventeen of them, all sizes and shapes. I thought they were rather splendid making the effort to come so far. The guardsmen loved it and as usual behaved very badly making rude remarks at the wrong moment. We gather they had been treated rather badly elsewhere, they said nobody bothered to speak to them, and they were segregated away, given meals in tents by themselves. We filled them up with Pimms and gave them a slap up lunch and they were very appreciative. Ivie Benson gave Colonel Peter a tremendous kiss. (We reckoned it was the first kiss from a female he has had for several years!)

It is not the only honour he has received in the last few days. It has come through he was awarded an OBE in the Birthday Honours. We all feel it is justly deserved.

Later in the week we are all going down to Abu Sultan to guard the ammunition depot. The advance party left this morning. The battalion will be down there for a month. I expect you will remember Abu Sultan is a huge ammunition depot with ammunition bays spread out over a huge area. It's a 'God forsaken place' out in the desert. I gather it is most uncomfortable; apart from being extremely hot we live in concrete bunkers. At our briefing we were told each company has a separate area of responsibility. We will be doing endless patrols round the perimeter and guardsmen will do sentry duty most of the time. We have also been told it is number 1 on the Egyptian hot list to sabotage. There have been quite a number of incidents there in the last few weeks, so we can expect some excitements.

I will give you my plans for my leave. I return to Port Said on 20th June, pack my kit and then drive down to Fayid, stay the night with the Micks and fly the following day to Cyprus and meet Father, and then after a short stop over in the Canal Zone, fly down the Nile to Kenya on 27th. Two officers in the battalion are coming with me, James Ogilvy and Owen Varney. I think it will be great fun and I am much looking forward to getting away.

15th June 1954

Abu Sultan

We arrived here yesterday and took over from the York and Lancs. They must be an extraordinary bunch of people. I hate grumbling but the whole place is in the most appalling condition. John Ramsay, my company commander, spent 24 hours with them; he said they were quite happy to live in filth and squalor. I have never seen such intensity of flies.

I don't know if you ever came here? It is just one vast area of desert with ammunition bays scattered in groups. The bays are almost submerged in the ground, all one can see are just bumps. We are three companies strong; each company has an area of responsibility. Our area is the smallest of the three; we have two and half miles of perimeter fencing to look after. Just the other side of the wire runs the Sweet Water Canal and beyond lies a very mangy plantation. However, we are told all the past trouble comes from our area. The saving grace is that we will be kept busy and expect the break-ins and excitements. To cover the area we have three look out posts and two very powerful searchlights. We also have to provide cable-cutting patrols. John said, "The joker in the pack is not the Egyptian thieves but the trigger happy RAF night guards who are very jumpy and unreliable". John told the RAF he wouldn't hesitate to return their fire with deadly accuracy if they opened up on us!

Abu Sultan is a perfectly vile place, made worse by the squalor the other units left behind... BTE don't care a damn ... Colonel Peter has raised hell with BTE, the staff couldn't understand his complaints as nobody had complained before. The attitude seems to be... "Damn swanky Guards regiment expects the red carpet and when they have to rough it... they complain!" We are evidently very unpopular with BTE as we keep pestering them about the awful state of this camp. All the hygiene arrangements are inadequate and, as a result the privates in the previous unit crapped anywhere they liked. Flies and stench everywhere.

There was a tremendous flap this morning. I was given the task of getting rid of the vast amount of rubbish in the company area... my platoon got it all into one huge pile, volumes of muck and filth. Most of the problems of the flies are caused by the filth, and you don't need much imagination to see the health risk. I found some old oil drums and we set the whole pile alight, it made a jolly good bonfire. After about ten minutes two characters from the RAOC shuffled over to see what I was doing. I told them I was burning the rubbish as it was a health risk. "Oh Sir, look at the ammunition bays." "Yes" I said. "One is 200 yards up wind and the other bay is 500 yards down wind." They stood there complaining. "If you people were doing your job - none of this filth would be here, either help me or go away. I have no intention of stopping this until it is cleared up." About five minutes later a Regimental Sergeant Major in the RAOC appeared in great alarm complaining of the danger caused by my fire. I gave him the same message as I had given his two friends. "The job is nearly complete and I have every intention of finishing it." I told him "I was astonished he allowed this area go get so filthy. If his unit were used to living in squalor, we certainly were not!" He went off muttering. About half an hour later, I had more or less finished, when our Company Sergeant Major appeared saying there was a general alarm. The officer commanding the BAD (Base Ammunition Depot) was in a complete flap and furious that anyone had lit a fire in his area. All available fire engines had been alerted and were on their way. The fire smouldered for a few minutes and then we covered up the last of the embers with sand. I had the satisfaction of watching all these fire engines racing round the desert unable to locate the fire. I expect there will be an inquiry and I shall labour the point that we were not prepared to live in such a filthy place.

I shall be delighted to leave this place next week, but it makes one realise the low standards, laziness and incompetence of most of the units in this part of the world.

21st June 1954

Headquarters, British Troops Egypt

Going back to where my last letter ended, from Abu Sultan. I left there last Thursday. It really was a beastly place. It was extremely hot most of the time and quite unpleasantly cold at night. Guarding ammunition dumps is about the most boring thing I can imagine. During the last few days we have been trying to catch the cable cutting thieves; I spent hours sitting out in a palm plantation waiting for some Egyptian thief to cut the cable and on another occasion I spent hours trying to hide in a Mohammedan grave yard, a terrible place, masses of pie dogs scavenging on human remains and bones which were littered all over the place. This has been a popular place for trouble, both by day and night. It is extremely difficult ever to catch them, as there are native villages, which overlook our area; they can see us miles away. They watch our patrols and move in when we are somewhere else. It is virtually impossible to keep the whole area under observation the whole time. They cut the cable two mornings ago, just before I left; John sent me to see if I could do anything, I went out at 3 am with three guardsmen and hid in an ambush, in a line of trees, till midday. It proved fruitless; it was extremely hot and uncomfortable. The following day another ensign, Peter Copeland, did the same. The cable was cut while he was in position but he had put himself in such a position he didn't see them. John was furious. So he went out the following night and exactly the same thing happened, the cable was cut right under our noses, behind another rise. When I left the saga continued ... they are very cheeky thieves - this lot!

Back to my travels. I returned to Port Said and left all my military kit and collected what I needed for Kenya. James Ogilvy, Owen Varney and myself drove south to Fayid and spent the night with the Irish Guards, where we met Warren, who had flown up from Kenya. The plan was that we flew out of Fayid at 7.00 and be in Cyprus by 8.30, but that was not to be! We got down to RAF Fayid. They were a most unhelpful and tiresome lot. They produced endless forms that had to be signed. Warren protested it was his plane he had brought up from Kenya. Nevertheless they were being perfectly bloody and refused to budge. Warren was told until the forms were correctly filled in they could not be cleared for take off. Warren produced some forms but the RAF were still not satisfied as Warren's forms were white and the RAF demanded them in pink! They also demanded the unit commander sign the documents, so we drove five miles down the road to the Grenadier Battalion and got Colonel Charles Earle to sign them while he was having his breakfast. It was after 10.30 before we were cleared for take off. I am afraid the Canal Zone does collect the most appalling cross section of humanity. For sheer bloody mindedness this incident took the prize.

Cyprus was a huge cultural shock; forty eight hours before I was lying in a plantation trying to ambush thieves, now we were enjoying the bright lights of Nicosia, We had dinner at The Gourmet Hotel and then made our way to the Chantier Clair, an open air night club. Owen had been there before. They had a reputation of having a very good cabaret and floorshow. It wasn't bad. They had some Spanish dancers who were excellent. We drank too much cheap Cyprus wine and felt ghastly next morning.

Then on Saturday morning, we planned to go round the island. Our first stop was an enchanting small monastery; the monks were most hospitable, we drank Coca Cola with them, and then they showed us round their garden and their abbey, which was a very ancient Byzantine building. It was a lovely setting. Can you visualise? In the foreground a bubbling mountain stream running through the garden with huge red and white clumps of oleanders on either bank. In the middle distance was the white washed monastery, Cyprus trees and fruit trees in abundance and then the fir clad mountains behind. Such a sight makes one's fingers tingle. Oh! If only I had time to paint it!

5th July 1954

c/o Father's house Muthaiga   GHQ East Africa PO Box 4000
Nairobi, Kenya

It's a week since I wrote and so much has happened. I have been on the move day and night. It's hard to know where to start.

I am sleeping in a caravan in the garden which is the same as I had last year. Brigadier Michael Carver, Peter Gillet and Warren are all living here. The house is run like a Mess but it is small and comfortable. There is a platoon outside on security duty.

The big event last week was the Nairobi race meeting on Saturday. The course is outside the town and was only built last year. It's very attractive. It has a magnificent grand stand with individual boxes on the top. The governor has one and we were invited to use his. Derrick Erskine, Lord Delamare and all the owners have their individual boxes and some are available for hire. It has a splendid paddock, very attractive and beautifully kept flowerbeds, and wonderful thick turf. The whole setting reminded me of a much prettier version of Hawthornhill, where we used to watch pony racing near Maidenhead.

Father took me to the American Consulate yesterday for their 4th July Independence Day party. The Governor toasted the President and the Consul toasted The Queen. A great deal of backslapping went on! I was amused to see the diplomatic community - such as it is here. All the official folk were there like the Mayor and the leading politicians. After the champagne we had lunch with General Slim Hymen, Father's chief of staff. They have got a house up the road, Hamilton House; it's strange stockbroker Tudor in the middle of Africa, more suitable in Sunningdale.

Father was busy this morning so I was lent a landrover and I drove about 30 miles to the edge of the escarpment and painted a picture. I sat on the edge of a cliff, looking across the whole of the Rift Valley to Mount Longonot - with half Kenya laid out like a patchwork quilt before me. Although it is a tremendous sight, it is not an easy subject to put on canvas. I was trying to capture a hundred square miles on a ten-inch square canvas. I came away rather frustrated and disappointed, as I could not do justice to the magnificent view.

Tomorrow, and for the next few days, Father has planned to take me on a tour with him, going round and seeing various units in the different parts of the country, mainly in the Kikuyu reserve and at all the hot spots. Meanwhile, intermingled amongst this activity are various dances, a SAFFA Ball, Lady Delamare's dance and a host of other parties. So one is on the move 24 hours a day with hardly time to take breath, and all this is happening during a war! The Mau Mau rebellion one has almost forgotten about till one sees the units with Father, engaged in combat. It is all vastly exciting and enjoyable. I have never enjoyed life so much.

6th August 1954

Government House
Dar-es-Salaam Tanganyika

This is the first time for three weeks I have had a chance to write and tell you of my adventures. I return tomorrow to Nairobi and have three days with Father and then fly back to the Canal Zone and my leave is over.

I am at a loss to know where to start and whatever I write will be a pale shade compared with the reality of all the places we have been to and things we have seen.

To start at the beginning, Owen and I arrived here on a flight from Arusha and met up with James who had flown down from Nairobi the same afternoon. The following day we set off in the Governor's party on a remarkable tour of the Southern Province of Tanganyika. I should explain it was a real circus. The whole party consisted of about eighty souls. There was a detachment of about 30 police who provided a Guard of Honour wherever the Governor stopped. There were about another 20 members of the Police band who played continuously at all the functions that occurred along the way. There were a host of Officials from the Provincial Commissioner and several District Commissioners and Colonial officials of every hue and cry, all their various minions from government departments mixed up with technical officers, medical officers, agricultural experts and civilian hangers on who had been invited. Then there were us, we were called 'The three military gentlemen.' I have not mentioned the number of drivers and servants brought along as every official had at least one servant with him. This huge gathering of people descended on the poor unsuspecting locals like some biblical event. I doubt if the Queen of Sheba in ancient times moved in greater splendour. We quite literally witnessed the British Colonial administration in its most glorious fashion. Here was the British Governor in all his power going out into the wildest parts of the Empire and bringing civilisation to the doorstep of the natives. I am sure they were vastly impressed. (If they were not, I certainly was!) Our liberal friends would be squirming in their shoes at such paternalism.

The Southern Province of Tanganyika is more or less the whole of the country south of Dar - es -Salaam. It's about the size of France. Our initial destination was Mtawara, which lies at the southernmost point of the country on the Rufugi River; beyond, is Portuguese East Africa. With British Government aid and other subsidies a new harbour had been constructed and a railhead created. This gave the Province a port, which was expected to bring new commercial activity and prosperity to the whole region. There were hardly any other buildings except a hotel, where we stayed; otherwise the landscape was all sisal plantations, stretching for miles. I gathered all Indian owned. We were witnessing a birth of a town. There was only one long berth and breakwater, one rather lonely railway line with one train standing in expectation!

It was a strange sensation, as one had to imagine that in a few years this would be a bustling port; almost nothing existed as we stood beneath the ship listening to a series of speeches on the perfect tropical evening. There were modest light eats and fruit juice and HE concluded the evening by conducting the police band to the delight of the crowd...

Every day the routine was much the same. The first to depart two hours ahead of the official party would be the police Guard of Honour with their band. They would form up on the village square, and then the officials would arrive and make their way to a prominent position and wait for HE's arrival. HE looked the quintessence of authority, dressed in white and wearing an impressive helmet with cock's feathers, accompanied by several Commissioners also in white, and his ADC, in Royal Marine uniform. The band would play, 'God save the Queen'. He would inspect the Guard of Honour who then marched off. The official party would then go to the arranged position on the village square where the leading tribal personality would welcome HE and he would respond. His message was roughly the same . . . He was very pleased to be here and he brought special greeting from The Queen. He would say how pleased he was to hear about the various projects that the community were undertaking and he then listed what further help and financial assistance they could expect. Sometimes he showed disappointment that he heard that money had been wasted and reminded them they must do better, and he would return and hope the reports were improved. There would be more speeches thanking HE and sometimes there would be requests for further assistance in some project. Then gifts would be brought forward and presented by members of the tribe. The gifts were generally quite modest like a carved walking stick or some piece of handcraft. On one occasion a small stuffed crocodile was presented to HE; he turned and passed it to James who nursed it for the rest of the tour. *(It was not properly cured and when James got back to the Canal Zone it was stinking and sadly had to be thrown away.)*

Usually there would be some form of entertainment. Each tribe specialised in some different form of dancing and music. They would demonstrate their skills dressed in their own way. On one occasion they danced on stilts, and on another they were dressed in feathers and painted themselves looking very warlike. The official party would be given light refreshment, the police band would play for hours to the delight of the locals and at the end always HE would conduct the band in well rehearsed tunes, and the party would go on into the tropical night until the band departed.

We did several long detours into the interior stopping at a number of small towns and we also visited a number of small communities along the coast which were very different in character - essentially Arab as opposed to African. One special place fascinated me, it was called Kilwa. It had once been an important Portuguese trading base in the 17th century and a ruined castle was still evident, and in more recent times it had been a slave port, which the Zanzibar Arabs used in their horrific trade. Kilwa remained largely unspoilt and undeveloped. It had a horrible sinister atmosphere. The buildings looked dilapidated and deserted. One could well imagine slaves being brought in and dispatched to Zanzibar or Arabia. The beaches were deserted except for the old dhows that lay rotting on the beach, and there was hardly any sign of life except once a day a small fish market came to life. It was very paintable… but there was no time to linger and anyway I hadn't brought my paints on the tour.

In summing up, all I can say… it was amazing seeing so much of this country in the shadow of a remarkable Governor. At the centre of it was the leadership exercised by the Governor which filtered down the colonial chain. If anyone doubted the value of British Colonial rule this was an example of the dedication of British Colonial officials. Their work and influence was having an impact on a huge African population, bringing them into the civilisation that this country could be justly proud of. I was so lucky to have had the experience of being on this tour.

16th August 1954

Quebec Camp North Camp Moscar

This morning I got a wonderful surprise … your lovely gold tiepin arrived. How extremely kind and sweet of you. *(Mother had sent me a gold tiepin, as it was my 21st birthday on 20th August)* It arrived safely, and I am wearing it now. I have had several complimentary remarks from friends about how smart I am, as my tie is never pulled down, and now it is. Thank you again.

This week has been quite eventful and I have been busy. I should explain, the battalion is committed to doing Ismalia and garrison duties. Our company task is to do duty here, at Avery Camp. We are also the reserve company as if there is a problem in Ismalia, we are close at hand. We are at half an hour notice to move.

Two things this week, which were notable. First a practical joke I played on all the other officers here. Secondly, a party at the United Services Club, which you will remember. They are now very short of glasses, tables and chairs, but more of that later…

Colonel Peter Fane Gladwin left on Friday morning. There have been a series of farewell parties. There was a big do in the Mess which consisted of a very long dinner night with five pipers playing two sets and a special new tune, Colonel Fane Gladwin's Farewell in Egypt. *(There are quite a number of pipe tunes called after Regimental personalities. Most I suspect will never see the light of day again but there are a few which merit their place in the Regimental pipe tune book and one is Brigadier Malcolm Erskine's March. It is a good tune and is sometimes played.)* The following night there was a mammoth party in the Sergeants' Mess. Whisky flowed like water. The evening started off quite formally with a dinner and speeches and a presentation to Colonel Peter, which was very moving. The evening deteriorated into a somewhat rowdy singsong. Its hard to know from my perspective but it became apparent that Colonel Peter was a much loved Commanding Officer and he had commanded the battalion very well in very difficult circumstances. *(This was recognised as he was later awarded a DSO.)*

Then at nine next morning the Battalion lined up from the Officers Mess to the main gate and after saying good-bye to us all, a party of sergeants and colour sergeants led by the pipe band pulled his car to the Main Gate. Poor Colonel Peter was completely overcome, tears falling down his face as he finally left the gate. Nobody ever left Quebec so dismayed!

On the night of the Sergeant's Mess party, one officer had to stay behind on duty at Avery Camp. We tossed - I lost! Late in the evening I went round doing my last inspections and checking the Guard. Just as I was going to bed I noticed a huge puddle of water, a tap had been left on and water was everywhere. This had attracted thousands of frogs – croaking, croaking -- the noise was deafening. So I got a bucket and took my shoes off and set about catching them. I got the trick fairly quickly and before long I had several buckets full of a seething mass of these revolting bullfrogs. Then, I asked myself, what was I to do with them? I am afraid my evil mind quickly thought that I would put them in the rooms of the other officers.

The first bucket of frogs I put into Peter Copeland's room *(He was a new ensign in the company)*. I knew I was quite safe as I was sure the Mess party would go on late. I pushed these frogs into his washstand. In no time they were jumping all over his room. I turned out the light; the croaking began again. I got the second bucket and put these frogs in Donald Marr's room - much the same happened. They were jumping everywhere, into his cupboard, on his chair, under his bed, everywhere, croaking like mad, making a thunderous din! I got a third bucket and put them in Alistair Ritchie's room, (my company Commander. I think you met him with his uncle, Neil, in Singapore when he was staying.) I did exactly the same; I filled his rooms with frogs. I put 15 frogs into his washstand and I can assure you the sound of croaking vibrating inside was incredible. It went better than I expected ... they returned well after 1am, all very sloshed. Alistair actually got into bed before he heard the frogs and was amazed. His immediate reaction was to be furious and then he roared with laughter and went along to see if the others had any frogs in their room. He found Peter lying flat on his tummy trying to extract the frogs from under his bed. Donald was on his hands and knees trying to shoo them from under his chest of drawers. They were all pickled with whisky .... it must have been a wonderful sight. It never dawned on them it was me who was the devil. Next morning at breakfast they were telling each other of the horrors of the night before. "One damn little bugger even got into my bed." I kept a very straight face and said nothing for a few days.

This letter continues 21st August 1954

On Saturday night we had a big party - there were six of us, (James Ogilvy, David Walter, Patrick Cobold, myself and three others.) It started normally enough; we had an indifferent dinner at the US Club. Later we went to the bar to collect some drinks and found a number of very noisy Gunner subalterns from 41st Field Regiment. (They were stationed opposite us in North Camp; we had got to know some of them.) It was all quite harmless, they were singing and we joined in and then it was suggested we do a 19 some reel. Some of the gunners took over the band, much to the anger of the Air Force and their very refined ladies! (Some really dreadful looking women who shouldn't be allowed in an Officers' club. Our Guardsmen do better.) The stage was tailor made for fun. Champagne coolers and fire buckets were found and the Air Force got wet! Our party moved down to the pier ... we weren't doing any harm, but soon the Air Force officers and their loving couples, started being objectionable. We evidently had disturbed their activity! They were helped into the water! While we were down on the pier the Gunners had pushed everything into the lake, all the furniture, tables and chairs. We had nothing to do with this part of the evening but we were still on the pier when somebody said the Military

Police are here arresting everybody. We made a quick exit into the Right Flank Camp, which was adjacent to the club and waited there. Some of the Gunners came with us. We were soon besieged by the Military Police. We gave our sentries strict instructions that no Military Police are allowed into the camp. They hovered around for several hours. I heard the manager say there were twenty of us but when the MPs came everybody had gone ...

Of course, the incident has been grossly exaggerated and police reports have been flying round. The official view in the battalion is a good, very amusing party, but you must pay for damage. £E126. The wretched manager has put all his losses on to it and we are refusing to pay; I think we will have to pay about 30/- a head. Quite a way to celebrate my 21st birthday!

When do we all return home? God knows! There are rumours and rumours and the plans are changed again and again... We are told we are in the queue; the Marines and the South Lancs left last week. We are still hoping to be back by Christmas.

You would hardly recognise this part of Ismalia now. Devils Island gets smaller every day; the huge banyan tree nearby has gone. They are very cautious about removing guards too quickly. There has been the odd incident; three grenades were thrown into a holiday camp at Port Fuad last weekend and a bridge at Abu Sultan was completely destroyed by explosives, but the general feeling is that there is less pressure and overall, the terrorist activity has greatly lessened. The weather is still rather unpleasant ... hot and humid. Most afternoons are spent swimming at the beach next to the old French Beach, which is now in bounds again, but only for families. I saw Farouk's old yacht moored on Lake Timsha ... she looks filthy. Someone said she is used for taking pilgrims to Mecca.

27th August 1954

Quebec Camp
North Camp, Moscar

I generally have time to write one long letter a week. We have been kept quite busy most of the week. I expect you may be wondering what was the end of the US Club drama. Two days ago we were summoned to the Orderly Room by the Commanding Officer, (Colonel Tommy Bulkeley has recently taken over from Peter Fane Gladwin.) The Adjutant read out the police report slowly and seriously - our hearts sank! Then Colonel Tommy said "Well done, I wish I had been there!"

The report made very amusing reading. One Group Captain who was there with his mistress, kept a log of events. It read like this... " At 21.05 hours. I observed buns being thrown. 21.10 hours I observed a number of officers playing musical instruments. 21.15 hours I heard obscene songs being sung from the bar. 21.20 hours a group of very drunk officers took over the dance floor and shouted obscene Scottish oaths at each other. Many patrons left in disgust, and in fear of their safety. Patrons were being thrown into the lake by drunken officers 21.30 hours. The situation worsened, there was chaos on the dance floor, patrons and their ladies were soaked with water; and the drunken officers were throwing everything into the Lake. 21.35 hours the Military Police were called to restore order...." The only person who was taken away by the MPs was the poor unsuspecting Commanding Officer of 41st Field Regiment who had arrived later and had no knowledge of the party... He was very browned off!

The bill was knocked down from £E 120 to £E 75. We still refused to pay as we were convinced we were being taken for a ride and the manager had put down all his deficiencies for the past months and much of the list was complete fabrication. The Gunner colonel detailed his officers to individual tasks. One got the menu stands repaired, another obtained ashtrays. (I think he nicked them from the US Club in Fayid!) Another got chairs cheaply mended in Ismalia. In the end we paid £2 each, which we thought was reasonable.

Our old friends The Beds and Herts, who are now in the camp just opposite us in North Camp, have been having great celebrations to commemorate the 250th anniversary of the Battle of Blenheim. Last Friday and Saturday our Corps of Drums and Pipe Band with their band 'Beat the Retreat'. They had a huge cocktail party on Saturday night and half the Canal Zone was invited. They took over from 2 Para about two months ago when they went home. At the back of their Mess they have a garden with three dead palm trees. Here lies an interesting story. There has been a frightful row over these palm trees. Apparently their commanding officer (2 Para) told several young officers to go and get three palm trees to decorate their garden. Without any further instructions they found three palm trees growing somewhere in the desert in the middle of nowhere, sawed them off at the roots, loaded them onto a truck and brought them back to the Mess - as pleased as punch. For about a month they looked fine but as you can imagine the leaves turned brown and wilted and looked dreadful. The unit left to go home but meanwhile all hell broke. The Egyptians claimed each tree was worth a fortune. The young officers apparently had cut down five trees and left two behind. It was claimed that they got £E 200 worth of dates a year off each tree and over the next five years they claimed a £E 1000 for each tree. The row is still going on but as 2 Para are now in England and are refusing to pay, nobody here is accepting the claim. I imagine the Egyptians will get very little satisfaction.

2nd September 1954

Quebec Camp
North Camp, Moscar

The US Club is back to normal! We all paid £E2 each and flatly refused to pay a penny more. It was accepted without fuss. Two days ago I went and played tennis there, I was amused to find the marker who was the same person who used to come and play at the house. I asked him if he remembered and I had a long story how wonderful the General was, and what a wonderful Lady mother was. After playing tennis we went to get a drink and were faced with long faces; Emanuel the barman said. "You very bad men! You are in big trouble with fundi." We told them we would be back on Saturday evening. Later we heard the MPs had been alerted for Saturday night!

Yesterday I went and watched the Guard Mounting at the Stadium, just outside the NAAFI. We laid on a very impressive show; both our Pipe Band and Corps of Drums took part. Most mornings the Pipe Band takes part of the Guard down to Queen's Gate, the Corps of Drums takes the remainder to Flagstaff House, but on this occasion the Adjutant, mounted on a large grey horse - looking tremendous - led both bands to Queen's Gate. When they got to the Gate, on the road outside the AKC building, the bands played alternately, during the Changing of the Guard. The two guards presented arms and the Old Guard marched back up the Mall. *(The main road running through Moscar.)* It was very impressive and a huge crowd gathered, and scores of children followed the guard. The Police Sergeant had his time cut out trying to stop the children from getting under the Adjutant's horse. Giles would have loved it!

15th September 1954

Quebec Camp North Camp, Moscar

Quite an amusing story... A strong man turned up at the camp gates the other day announcing he was an entertainer. He was wearing a yellow shirt, riding breeches, high boots, covered in rings and thick leather bands round his arms. A very odd sight indeed. He demanded to see the Commanding Officer. The Sergeant of the guard had the wit to get hold of Owen *(Varney)* who is designated the entertainments officer. He took him off to the Orderly Room where Michael FitzAlan Howard, the Second in Command, was the only person there at the time. Owen marched in and said "I have a strong man who would like to see you, Sir." Michael asked this character what he could do? He wanted to put on a show and bring with him his tummy dancers, gully gully men and his trapeze artists. "I have the best tummy dancers in Egypt. I give you a good show. I make you laugh. I give you sexy display." There followed a certain amount of discussion over the contract and the date was fixed for next Tuesday.
This was not the end of the story. After the Orderly Room meeting, Owen

said to this character he didn't think he was a strong man. His outfit was just all for show. The strong man pretended to be highly indignant. He picked up a stone slab, which was lying on the ground and placed it on his head and told Owen to get an axe and with the blunt end he could smash the slab into pieces. This bizarre demonstration was done in front of Owens's machine gun platoon; there was tremendous applause, Owen took a tremendous swing - crash, the stone slab was completely shattered. The man blinked, shook his head and was unaffected! There was more applause! He then handed out photographs of himself and his tummy dancers. Owen said he had quite some difficulty getting rid of the man out of the barracks.

I am kept quite busy, as I have been appointed the battalion education officer; I hasten to add anyone less suitable to teach guardsmen would be hard to find. In reality I have to organise others to do the donkey work; there is an intensive course for 2nd Class exams at the end of the month. Each company has to organise the 3rd Class tuition as there are so many and the individuals are difficult to concentrate due the guard duties and other commitments. It amazes me the low level of education of most guardsmen when one considers that education is compulsory in England.

26th September 1954

1st Battalion Scots Guards MELF 26

Since I last wrote the great news has been announced the Battalion leaves Egypt on 11th December. They say it is a 90% certainty; it is quite likely to be a day or two either way but the big thing is that we will be home for Christmas. Everybody's spirits are very high and at last we know how much longer we are doing duties, etc; before there was nothing definite and we were expecting a date early in the New Year.

One's life revolves round the duty roster which has been the case as long as the battalion has been committed to Port Said duties and now down here doing Ismalia and Moscar duties. We don't have a platoon that we get to know and work with and train. Young officers in the company take rifle inspections, undertake the company chores such as supervising education but sadly never have a chance of developing a well-trained platoon. Guardsmen are in theory allotted to platoons, but the platoon commanders never see them as a group; they are also on a duty roster which bears no relationship to the platoons they are in. There is almost no time for training and getting to know one's men. The battalion is run from the Orderly Room. It is not a very satisfying form of soldering.

I mentioned in an earlier letter about a strong man who appeared and offered to do a show. Well, he came on Tuesday and brought his tummy dancers, which turned out to be a tremendous success. The guardsmen thought it was the best thing they had ever seen. The dancers were ghastly old bags of 40 plus, but it was extremely funny. They brought a very corny three piece band consisting of a base drum which was held in place by broken bricks, a side drum and an old trumpet. The only tune they could play was 'It's a long way from Tipperary'. They played it continuously for two hours. There was a little man who balanced things on his head. At one point he tried to balance a bicycle on his forehead but the wheels hit the tent roof and it all came down with a crash! The strong man was very entertaining. There are a number of guardsmen into bodybuilding - lifting and heaving heavy weights; this character was right up their street. He bit a six-inch nail in half, (it was a genuine one produced by the pioneers.) He bent a horseshoe double. He had a large tombstone broken on his head and another on his stomach. He pinned a broach on himself sticking the point through his throat and then walked round displaying it. I think he was given £E 100 for his trouble.

The lights keep going out, this letter has been written by candlelight and is very disjointed; the breeze keeps blowing out the candle… it's a bit of a struggle making any sense.

14th October 1954

Quebec Camp
North Camp Moscar

We have moved up to Abu Sultan, which hasn't changed one iota since we were there in June, except it is much cooler and less unpleasant. There was only one difference this time; all the companies were together in a central camp rather than being deployed round the whole area living in very uncomfortable conditions. I don't know whether it was more effective but it was certainly less hardship for the guardsmen. Not long ago there was a big break-in, a whole camel train came in through the wire and took a mass of large 17lbs shells; when they got outside the perimeter, they gutted them all and only took away the brass shell cases. While we were there nothing happened. We came back here on Wednesday and are back doing Ismalia duties again for a month. The advance party leaves tomorrow. We are dreading that a dock strike will delay our return. Everybody is in tremendous heart; for many it will be the end of a three-year tour.

3rd November 1954

North Camp, Moscar

Time is passing at a tremendous rate ... all what I call 'going home signs' are beginning to take place. The measuring up for Home Service Clothing, MFO boxes are being produced, stores are being packed. Battle dress is now in wear rather than KD. The number of times this battalion has come to Egypt and left thinking for the last time, the first being in 1801. *(In less than two years the British Army was back in Egypt during the Suez crisis in October 1956. The battalion was not involved on this occasion.)*

The Canal Zone is now almost as it was when you were here before the trouble started. There seem to be very few incidents; those that do occur are theft in nature rather than terrorist inspired. Ismalia is in bounds again. All the guard positions are coming down one by one. Ten days ago when I was on duty at Avery Camp I helped to dismantle Devil's Island. Today the guard comes off the Agricultural Building and that was dismantled this morning. An old lady came up to Nigel Porter who was directing operations, almost weeping saying how sad she was to see us go. I think she was from the Nunnery nearby. So much has changed in the last weeks. We no long need an escort, we can go almost anywhere now by day or night - that is if one has the transport.

Last Monday I went up to Port Said - on a swan - doing jobs for others. Mother always said Port Said held a tremendous fascination to her, I agree. When we were there, living in a camp behind the slums and next to their prison, it was just a filthy place but driving round the streets near the harbour one appreciates its charm. I went round seeing all the old shopkeepers who we used to know so well and drinking Coca Cola with them. They were all there, smiling as ever, and trying to sell one everything! We sat and had an ice cream. In the past one asked for a President Neguib, (much the same as we used to ask for a King Farouk at Groppies.) Now the ice cream is a President Nasser! We lunched at Acri, the restaurant at the top of the building overlooking the whole town. We heard that there was a shooting incident in the main street the other day. Several Ikwan were involved and two locals were killed. One imagines a bit of blood letting.

Next week is going to be rather fun. General Hull has very kindly asked me to go to the Florence Nightingale Ball in their party. Then later in the week is the 32nd Guards Brigade Party. There have been a series of rows about farewell parties. The idea being to have one party and ask everybody from far and near. Anyway, what eventually has happened is we are now having our own after the Brigade Party. Tummy dancers, striptease artists, roulette - everything, may be rather mad, but much more fun.

6th December 1954

Quebec Camp .
North Camp Moscar

The end of Egypt is in sight, we leave here on 11th December... Everything is so uncomfortable now. There has been a tremendous rush to hand everything into the storage depot. We have lost our transport, all the furniture went yesterday and all our kit and MFO boxes go tomorrow so we just live in our tents with only our beds. We are handing over the camp to the RASC next door. The RASC divisional column and our camp are just going to increase the size of their camp. The Beds and Herts camp opposite was sold two days ago. You have never seen such a sight in your life. Every down and out Egyptian from all over the country appeared in their thousands with camels, donkeys and a mass of old broken down vehicles, anything to transport their spoil away. In the middle of the barrack square were an Egyptian and a British auctioneer selling everything down to the last sheet of corrugated iron, old oil drums, piles of scrap wood and masses of fencing wire, even old rope; the last bit of rubbish had some value. You have never seen such filth but it all made money. In two hours the camp just disappeared.

The end of last week we had our last Battalion shooting match. It was great fun. There were three teams, officers, sergeants, corporals and guardsmen. Each team consisted of eight and the total scores were added together. The officers won by 40 points, the guardsmen won the falling plate competition. Then the following day we had an individual competition, nearly everybody took part. Tony Boam, the weapon training officer won. The Pipe Major was second; I was 14th out of 65.

We have been running day trips to Cairo for the guardsmen and it's been a tremendous success. We have had several weeks of negotiations. First, we asked the Y, M.C.A; they passed us on to Cooks who quoted £E4 a head which was considered too much. Then we asked Missary, the Egyptian shipping company, to quote. We knew they have very good buses and we said we wanted no frills, just to Cairo and back with one guide; they quoted £E2 a head. Last Friday was the first trip. Our Guardsmen were the first British troops to visit Cairo since the troubles in 1951. I have never seen such a Public Relations bonanza. The Daily Mirror arranged a special lunch party. Everywhere the guardsmen went in Cairo the press followed them, several were asked to make statements, one was asked to do a recording, they were photographed the whole time. There was a huge full spread in the Egyptian Gazette; the BBC ran the story on their world service and it was a sensation here in the Canal Zone. They went to all the usual places, the Citadel, the Mohamed Ali Mosque in the morning and after lunch to the Pyramids, finishing at Gropes. A second party went on Saturday and a third on Sunday. I didn't put my name down as I have seen all the sights but I might go if there is an officer party before we leave. Everybody who has been says the Egyptians are making every effort and nothing is too much trouble. One can hardly believe the change of events. The political climate has changed dramatically.

10th December 1954

Quebec Camp
North Camp, Moscar

On Wednesday morning at 8.00 someone burst into my tent and asked me if I would like to go to Cairo in a taxi, which was leaving in 15 minutes! I accepted, but I had to travel under the name of Major Tony Phillipson who was going and suddenly couldn't and the pass was made out in his name and couldn't be changed, so I had to pretend I was a major! So at 8.15 with only £E5 in my pocket off we set.

After all the fuss about passes we weren't asked for our passes once on the way up. Even at Tel el Kabir where there is huge roadblock as it is the end of the Canal Zone, the police waved us straight through. We felt it was a considerable achievement getting to Cairo in a private party, as it is still not officially open till next week.

We have travelled that road so many times in the past, it was quite moving to be on that road again and so little has changed. *(At the beginning and end of every summer holidays we drove along the road when my parents fetched us from the airport or later took us back. We did several short stays in Cairo during the three years my parents were there, also using the road.)* Some of the gum trees had been felled and there were several military emplacements, but otherwise the congestion of native transport on the narrow road was exactly the same.

We arrived in Cairo at 11.00; we dropped our cases at The Semeramis Hotel where we were booked in. The Semeramis has been doing tremendous business since Shepherds was burnt down a year or two ago.

The Continental and Mena House have been sold and changed hands and we understand have gone downhill. Now everybody goes to The Semeramis, which has a wonderful position overlooking the Nile. We were told the Americans are going to build a Hilton on the site of the old British barracks at Kaiser el Nil which had already been demolished. Shepherds is being rebuilt on a new site.

I have always been fascinated by Cairo. It has its own special smells, a grandeur mixed with squalor, it exudes age, and its ancient buildings reflect the layer upon layer of different cultural mixes. It has its own type of oriental magic, not least, some very happy memories when you used to take us there to stay. The centre of Cairo is in an awful mess as the main streets are all dug up and they are laying cables under the pavements and, as a result, one has to walk in the road which is congested and highly dangerous.

The first thing we did was to rush off to the Pyramids. We had lunch at Mina House and then after lunch we decided to climb them. Something I have always wanted to do. It took us exactly 30minutes to go up; we hung around at the top for a little while, long enough to write ERSKINE on the top stone amongst 30,000 other names and then came down and retired to Mina House for a drink. Mina House looked awfully gloomy and had a horrid atmosphere so we decided to recover at Gropes which was quite wonderful as always. Do you remember how we used to order King Farouk ice creams? We ordered a President Nasser ice cream and it was exactly the same!

We had dinner at The Semeramis and oddly enough sitting at the next table was Cark Davis, your old American friend who used to pull your leg about artificial fertilisers. He was with his wife so I went up to him afterwards and spoke to them for quite a long time and they asked after you. He gave me lunch the following day. He is a most interesting man; he said he was in Cairo negotiating a project in Sinai - I think oil. He has been seeing Nasser and all the top people. He was very interested to hear about Father in Kenya and he asked after Polly.

Another person I saw by accident at The Semeramis was Martin Turner who is head of De La Rue's foreign sales department. He came up to me at the bar and asked if I was Bobby's Boy? "Yes Of course" I said He said he had just come from Nairobi where he had had dinner with Father the night before. We talked about De La Rues for some time and he very kindly gave me a set of their new cards. I will keep them for you.

We had a very amusing evening. We ended up at Farouk's old haunt, Auberge du Pyramid. I think it must be one of the kinkiest places on earth; you had to be very drunk or nearly mad to enjoy it, but after a year in the desert I think our sanity was ripe for watching that kind of activity. We got back to our hotel at 3.00 am and after a late start we did the tourist rounds, first to The Citadel then to the Mohamed Ali Mosque and then on to the Muski. I didn't buy anything. (I was already broke and had to borrow to pay my hotel bill.) In the afternoon we went to the Cairo Museum and ended up again in Gropes. Just before we left the city, everybody had a mad desire to see the Sphinx by moonlight. It was a full moon. When we got there they lit up the Sphinx with magnesium bombs. What a treat! It was fascinating and beautiful beyond imagination. We arrived back at Moscar at 12.30 exhausted and broke but having had a wonderful 36 hours.

Today I am piquet officer. To morrow morning we are taken to Port Said by train and we embark at midday. I hope to see you on the evening of 20th. It's quite wonderful to see the last of Egypt!

17th December 1954

On Board MV Georgic
With 1st Battalion Scots Guards

By the time you get this letter, I shall be at home, but at the moment there are three days of the voyage left.

Much has happened during the last week. I had a very entertaining and amusing 36 hours in Cairo: the final packing up of Quebec Camp and our farewell to Egypt and the voyage back. My big news is that Colonel Tommy told me yesterday that I would go as a Platoon Commander to

Pirbright. I am quite pleased about this, it has many advantages, among which one does a bit of soldering with a platoon, which one trains and takes right through their 12 weeks of training; it also entails taking them up to Yorkshire for two weeks. Whereas in a Battalion in London one is just another ensign on the piquet and guard roster and, apart from the odd visit to Thetford or Pirbright, one would never see the company at all. Colonel Tommy said he was sorry to send me away but he had to produce two regular ensigns, one for Pirbright, which was I, and the other for the Battle Training Camp at Pickering in Yorkshire. *(That was Patrick Cobold.)* There were no other regular ensigns. How long will I stay at Pirbright? I don't know, but I have to report there sometime in February. It's a change of scenery and after the effort of settling down I am sure I will enjoy Pirbright a lot. I always rather dreaded the idea of London although I would have liked to have done London duties for a short time; maybe I will get the chance later. I am also saved the expenses of London but I do think a car at Pirbright is vital. The other advantage is that I am much closer to home and the drive down to Cheriton and Mother is much closer.

The final week at Quebec Camp passed very quickly, uneventful and uncomfortable. Last Saturday morning the Battalion paraded on the square with a platoon of 3 tonners drawn up on the far side. After being inspected, each company mounted their transport and were driven down through Moscar. A large number turned out to wave us good-bye and there was a lot of cheering and a special loud cheer as we went past Queens Gate where the Welsh Guards had turned their guard out. The battalion debussed at the railway siding near the AKC building. The Welsh Guard band was there to play us away and many of their officers and other officers from BTE were also there. It was all rather moving. I think there was a general sadness to see us leave and a warmth had developed between our battalions; the Welsh Guards had been our neighbours for many months and we shared our duties and entertained each other at all levels.

It is the first and last time I ever travelled on a train in Egypt. It was rather strange seeing the very familiar sights from a different perspective. The train took us up the quay; we were put on a landing craft and taken out to the ship. The Grenadier Battalion band played us away. We did not in fact sail out of Port Said until dusk. It was a wonderful sight; the lights of Port Said came on, our pipe band played as we moved slowly out to the open sea, past De Lessep's statue, the Grenadier music faded away. There was hardly a dry eye on the ship.

The voyage so far has been very quiet and uneventful. Just nine days waiting around. The sea has been calm except for the second day out when we got into quite a swell and most people felt average sick. The Georgic is a good size ship but we are very crowded with a large number of troops on board, including The Buffs, (who have come up from your part of the world,) the Beds and Herts, also Brigade Headquarters and their hangers on. I share a cabin with three others. I expect you can well imagine what goes on the whole time. The mornings are taken up by doing drill. They don't like us stamping about on the deck! So it is very limited drill for guardsman and sword drill for the officers, PT some mornings and lectures. Then in the evenings either a film; we had Quo Vadis the other night, or roulette and the occasional dance. There are very few girls on board so it not much of a party.

This is rather a rambling letter but I feel, if I don't write now while it is still calm - we enter the Bay at 10 tonight - I would never finish it. We had a wonderful view yesterday when we passed Gib and Tangiers. We were more on the Tangiers side and we could see the coast so clearly.

Bu the time this letter arrives it will be Christmas. I do hope you will have a happy Christmas; I only wish I could be with you - dear Father - I know you won't have a dull Christmas staying with the Twinings. Give them my love.

The Colonel of the Buffs gave a very interesting lecture about Kenya the other night. A company commander and platoon commander both followed him describing the features and problems they encountered in the tour of duty; they were all very complimentary about you. Sadly I don't see how I can get out to you again. My plans are to go straight down to Somerset and see Mother and later may be have a few days with Eric; I am due back at Wellington Barracks on 24th January.

I never posted and finished this letter, so I will bring you up to date. Last night we docked at 7.00pm and there to meet us on the quay at Liverpool were about everyone who had served in the Battalion in the past three years. The Major General, Vernon Erskine Crum, The Lieutenant Colonel, Colonel Peter Fane Gladwin, Michael FitzAlan Howard and many others including James Ogilvy. Unfortunately the bar was dry, no drinks were being served but a few bottles appeared and everyone was well entertained. There was a certain amount of hanging around and eventually a train appeared and we were in London soon after 11.00pm. I was lucky to catch the last train down here.

I was so thrilled to get home - home at last. Mother was looking wonderful and Robert was away at some dance. Its lovely to be back...

Postscript

It's fifty years since I wrote these letters. The year in Egypt was an important landmark in my life. I made very light of serving on active service and the hardships were more than compensated by the comradeship of one's brother officers. I say with no exaggeration, we were a very efficient battalion and we justly earned a great reputation in Egypt. I never met a smarter Adjutant than Neil Ramsay or a more formidable Regimental Sergeant Major than Bob Thomson. Both Colonel Peter and Colonel Tommy were dedicated commanding officers. They stamped something very special on our lives, which was greatly treasured. I found myself Adjutant of the battalion four years later, and I could appreciate the demands on these officers. They welded us into a team and one owes a great deal to their example of leadership.

I look back with my life behind me; it was a wonderful experience to have served in the 1st Battalion in Egypt during 1954.

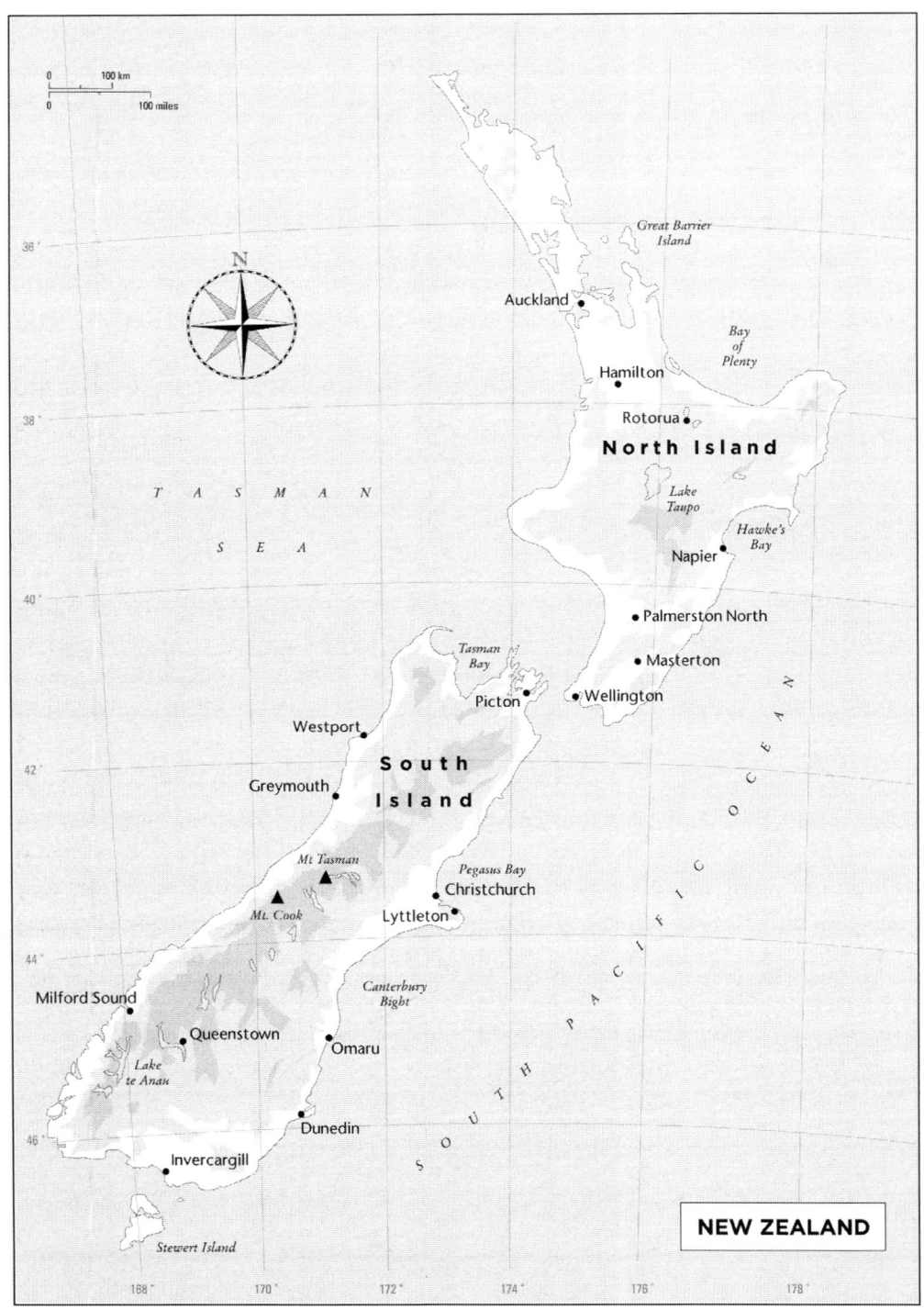

Section B

ADC to the Governor General, New Zealand 1959/1960

In April 1959 Philip Erskine was invited by the Regiment to consider the appointment of ADC to Lord Cobham, the Governor General of New Zealand, beginning that August. He readily accepted and, after taking over from Blair Stewart-Wilson, served for a year until September 1960. There were two ADCs on the Governor General's staff, the second being appointed from the Royal Navy.

Philip's duties as an ADC involved all the normal tasks associated with a staff officer to a senior diplomatic post: support to the Governor General at home or on tour; management of social events and help to the family. That Philip made the most of his year in Wellington is clear from his letters and that it was in New Zealand where he had both the opportunity and the wish, that his love of painting blossomed.

Philip was already engaged to Fiona Radcliffe before he went to New Zealand and the letters in this section were written exclusively to her. Fiona was by then living in South Africa where her parents had a house near Somerset West. On leaving Wellington in September 1960 Philip flew directly to South Africa where Fiona and he were married before Christmas. Thereafter he continued to serve in the Scots Guards until retiring in 1971 and moving permanently to live at the Cape.

Abbreviations. HE – His Excellency, ie the Governor General.
GH – Government House.

SETTLING INTO GOVERNMENT HOUSE

Government House, Wellington.   27th August 1959.

This is my first letter from New Zealand. Before this letter gets deeply into my arrival I must tell you on the last leg of my journey from Auckland airport, as I was waiting for my connection, I saw in front of me a familiar face, and he advanced towards me. It was Richard Cregeo who was with his boss Frankie Spite, so we travelled down together. I saw him again this evening when Blair *[Stewart-Wilson]*, my predecessor, and Neil Durden Smith gave a farewell party. I didn't have much chance to talk to him as he was off early on the ferry to Christchurch. I arrived at Wellington airport and was met by the GH chauffeur. I found everything as I would have expected. I was given a warm welcome by the Cobhams who couldn't have been more charming and friendly.

I was thrust immediately into the deep end as that night was the annual diplomatic reception. There were 150 diplomats from 25 countries that NZ does business with. Some of the diplomats were dressed up in an amazing way looking straight out of an opera. There was one character who had gold braid everywhere, round his arms, round his waist, his neck and about the only place where there was no braid, was where he was wearing his medals. Some were hanging short, some hanging long, some dangled – some didn't… He had a smile that sent a shiver down one's spine. I wouldn't trust him an inch…but I was told he was the pillar of diplomatic society.

My first impressions are that this is a very happy house. There are masses of children, (the Cobhams have eight but only six were here at that moment.) Everything is fun and not a fatigue. Everything is done on the lines of how to avoid being pompous. I have also been struck by the beauty of the country and everybody I have met so far has been really friendly so you mustn't worry about me……

Section B - ADC to the Governor General, New Zealand 1959/1960

FIRST IMPRESSIONS

Dated 29th August.

Blair Stuart-Wilson, my predecessor, left yesterday after lunch and is flying back. The new Naval ADC arrives in three weeks, and then the new team will be on our own. Lady C goes back to England in about three weeks and takes Jennie, her Lady in Waiting, and doesn't return till Christmas. There is no one taking over from Jennie till next June. I don't see myself being the huge success that Blair has been but he has left me copious notes and given me a very good briefing. I think he leaves a lot of broken hearts behind.

I am beginning to get to know my way round Government House and how it works. They say this building is the largest wooden construction in the world….. There is a grand entrance where one ADC spends most of the day welcoming guests and taking them through, either to HE in his study or the main reception room before meals. Our office is rather gloomy but convenient near the entrance. The walls are covered with photographs of former ADCs going back more than a hundred years. We each have our own desk, there are several cabinets of files, and a drink cupboard. The Lady in Waiting has a room on one side; it's a cosy room where there is always a warm cup of coffee and people tend to congregate. At the other end of the passage is HE's office, and then a small room for Lady C and then the big drawing room. The official staff live in a wing. My direct superior is the Military Secretary, Jock Harrison. He is a very decent but sad soul who is still suffering from the loss of his wife. Dave Fouhy is the Official Secretary, he has an assistant, John Purvis and his secretary, Kitty Woods. It all seems to work smoothly.

A CHRISTCHURCH VISIT

Clarendon Hotel, Christchurch.   Letter dated 29th August.

We flew down from Wellington this morning to Christchurch by a Dakota out of the Governor General's flight. We flew down the South Island coast and it was perfect weather and we got an excellent view of the country, and the mountains in the interior which were largely covered with snow. We were met at the airport by the usual party…Mayor, etc, and went straight to the Clarendon Hotel, and then on to watch the Rugby International: the Lions versus the All Blacks at Lancaster Park. This is serious stuff, and an amazing spectacle watched by a huge crowd of 65,000. There was never any doubt that the All Blacks would win, the final score was 8 – 21. In the evening I went with HE to a somewhat indifferent drinks party. We stayed for about an hour. I am amazed by how terribly friendly and charming everybody is and the hospitality is fantastic and seems eternal. I think it is a reflection of the popularity of the Cobhams. It is obvious they are well liked and doing a very good job.

PS Dated 31st August.

I was rather touched as I had a brief word with the Prime Minister, Mr Nash. He went out of his way and came over and spoke to me. He was very nice and cheerful and welcomed me to New Zealand. That was kind of him. Our flight back to Wellington was uneventful and we had another glorious view of the snow capped mountains.

CUTTING MY TEETH AS AN ADC.

Government House, Wellington.   3rd September 1959.

It's a great danger to measure everything by English standards, or to think in terms of social standards. I keep saying to myself I must not compare New Zealand with England. While there is much that we have in common with New Zealand: standards are different, circumstances are different, the country is different; everyone is extremely kind and nothing irritates them more than being patronised. You know this, I am sure, but I have to bear this in mind the whole time. I am very fortunate to be here; my job, in simple terms is to be part of a team to support the work of the Governor General.

Letter dated 4th September.

My last job is to go round making sure all the lights are turned out. It's quite a creepy place and being all wood there is a lot of creaking. I have a nice bedroom upstairs looking down the main lawn and a lovely picture of you over my dressing table, which keeps my morale up! One of the footmen is supposed to look after me but he does as little as he can get away with. There are three footmen, all 'gay' quite painful…but I am told they are all that will do the job.

Letter dated 7th September 1959.

I seem to have been kept busy almost non-stop. I am trying to teach myself to type. There is a type writer in our office and I thought I should use it…but I am very slow and make a great many mistakes. Now for my news. I wrote a long letter two nights ago. We had a big dinner party on Thursday of an assorted group. A judge, two businessmen, a man from Shell, a Rugby board member, a racing personality and an honorary ADC and all their wives. A somewhat 'pompous do'. I should explain that a dinner like this follows a set routine. One ADC meets the guests at the front door and with the help of the footmen they are shown into the large drawing room and given a drink. At about 8 o'clock the other ADC brings HE and Lady C down the stairs and the two ADCs do the presentations. It is vital that the ADC on duty in the drawing room gets the guests in the right order. Both ADCs have learnt the names of the guests by heart in that order. (I lie in the bath beforehand learning the names – word perfect!) As you will appreciate the ADC who accompanies HE down the stairs has not even seen the guests. But sometimes the guests, generally two women who know each other break ranks at the last minute and then the presentations go wrong and HE is not amused! The 'placement' is always done by Dave Fouhy, the Official Secretary, as he knows who is important. There is only a very limited official order of precedence, and only Dave understands the sensitive order of precedence within the business community. At the end of dinner Lady C gets up and leads the ladies out of the room, each making a curtsey to HE at the door as they leave. HE doesn't generally linger very long over his port and then he takes them all to join the ladies. Strangely enough it always goes quite smoothly. The next task of the ADCs is to bring up to HE and Lady C the next two important guests, say numbers 3 and 4. The male guests to Lady C and the female guests to HE. This is then repeated after about ten minutes with the next two pair of guests, until all the guests have been taken up. One has to watch carefully so as to avoid a situation where either HE or Lady C are struggling. It all normally works like clockwork. Generally HE and Lady C return after the guests have gone and there is a post mortem on the evening. Everybody relaxes and has a good giggle!

On Friday we had 120 Boy Scouts to receive the Queen's Medal from HE and then a reception afterwards. I am sure they are all very worthy people but I am allergic to Boy Scouts. I was once a Boy Scout at my prep school……I think I had done something to anger the scout master, and a notice was posted saying "Lord Baden Powell no longer required my services.."

Letter dated 7th September 1959.

I wrote a long letter this morning on the type writer. I didn't say all I wanted to. Its 11.00 pm. We have just had a long dinner. Lord C had a couple of old friends and there was a great 'bang on' and they talked about everything: Harold Macmillan to Worcestershire cricket; from Rhodes Scholars to South Africa; British Steel; world banking; hire purchase; back to cricket; Hitler and World War II. Meanwhile I was nodding my head in approval at the other end of the table… One guest was a certain Mr More who is the head of St Johns and the other guest, John Hare, the British Minister of Agriculture. I withdrew, left them to it.

Not much has happened today. I do find I have a great deal of time to twiddle my thumbs. One ADC has to be about even if nothing is happening in case of some emergency. I should explain at the bottom of the hill there is a large complex housing the local Technical College. I wandered down there to see if I could find something worthwhile… I discovered that they have life classes on Wednesdays and Thursdays so I booked myself in, starting next week. I know that I will find it difficult to be there every time but I should make it at least once a week. Drawing naked ladies will be a good form of relaxation after the hot house atmosphere of GH! I love the notion when asked what I do in my spare time.. fish, tennis or play golf, I will reply, in perfect truth: No, draw naked ladies!

I was asked by the Principal, who briefly interviewed me, if I was amateur or professional? If I was a professional artist I was admitted free but as an amateur I had to pay. I banged on for a few moments without giving an answer, but when he discovered I was from 'up the hill' at GH and a 'pommy' to boot, I was admitted free. Wasn't that nice! I would love to paint good portraits but one has to be accurate in one's drawing first… maybe with practice it will come. I am also looking forward to meeting the other students….

Extract from letter dated 10th September 1959.

It's ten in the evening. Three sailors are dining, a Rear Admiral and his entourage, so I thought I would go out leaving Neil to cope as it's a Naval affair. You may know this but it's almost impossible, so it seems, to get anything to eat in Wellington after 7 pm and there were no films I wanted to see. I eventually found a hot dog shop…….it's hard to believe that you could make a revolting hot dog but there appeared to be no alternative. It's a lesson I will remember.

I went to a timber merchant this afternoon and got some hard board and had it cut up into pieces, and have been busy painting and preparing them. The only place I can work is the garage and the chauffeur is terrified I am going to cover his cars with my paint! There is a little bit of tension building up.

My blood is tingling in a big way to get on and do some painting. All the gorse is out; the hills are golden yellow round Wellington and the evening lights are too wonderful. In a couple of days I shall have my boards ready. There are millions of subjects almost everywhere I look. I can drive out for an hour or two and work in the early morning; there will be no distractions.

I went down this afternoon briefly to check on the equipment I will need for my life classes. I only have to pay a small fee for the model of £2, which lasts till the end of November. I am really looking forward to my drawing.

I forgot to say we had an ecclesiastical lunch party today, with two cardinals and an archbishop. I was very impressed how HE marshalled his patter. One has to admit it's a great gift to turn on the right line of patter and charm to meet the vastly different audiences that appear. I do appreciate watching a master of this art at work. I sometimes ponder the value to myself of doing this job. Doing little more than be an upgraded footman, but one does have the privilege of being close to the centre of things of a nation. It's an extraordinary opportunity. I am sure in after life I will benefit from many lessons one has learnt. I might have been on the ranges training guardsmen, or commanding a company, but that will no doubt come along in due course anyway.

Government House dated 10th September.

I get rather taken aback by people telephoning, saying they have not yet received their invitation for the party tomorrow! One very pushy mother told me she always went to all Government House parties! I checked her name on the guest list and is wasn't on it…so I explained that HE made a point of inviting people who had not received invitations before and it in no way reflected on her, but that I know HE will be very pleased to hear 'you always support his events'. I think it is damn cheek! I gather it happens the whole time and when they get a refusal from one of the aides, they telephone the Military Secretary or Dave Fouhy, but I was warned not to give in but to be as polite as possible.

Section B - ADC to the Governor General, New Zealand 1959/1960

We had another large lunch party of 18 yesterday. It was billed as a working lunch as all the guests were here as part of the Board to discuss the Waitangai celebrations which happen every year to commemorate the signing of the Treaty of Waitangai between the settlers and the Maoris. The Prime Minister and several ministers were present. There was a very good atmosphere and HE is excellent at keeping the discussions going in a light and friendly way… there is always a possibility of difficulties.

In the morning I went with HE to the Executive Council meeting in Parliament. He attends it once a week. It corresponds to the Privy Council in England. A few years ago the New Zealand government abolished their upper house, the Senate. The Executive Council is an instrument which meets weekly with the Cabinet and the Governor General. He has to sign all the business that is going to come before Parliament. While it is largely routine, it is perceived that the Government cannot slip in any legislation that is unacceptable. The Governor General's powers have never been tested and HE thinks if he did refuse to sign, there would be a major constitutional crisis, and he would not win. So it's only another example of window dressing! The meeting only lasts 5 minutes but he sometimes lingers on and talks to the odd minister. I go in and announce him and then sit in the adjoining office with one of the parliamentary clerks who generally give me a cup of tea. HE dresses up in a top hat and morning coat, I try and look smart!

A DANCE AT GH.   THE NAVAL ADC'S DEPARTURE.

Government House dated 13th September 1959.

I will bring you up to date with my news. The dreaded dance was much more fun than I expected. I think in the end there were 250. It was a very mixed bag of local Wellingtonians, from the Prime Minister downwards. The band played well and there was a very good tempo going. The dance started at 9 and went on to about 1am when HE and Lady C withdrew. I tried to keep the 'wall flowers' dancing, which consisted mostly of the very young and the oldies…By and large everybody behaved very well but I was quite amused by the way the butler and footmen handled a few 'rowdies'. They came up behind them, one on each side and gently lifted them off the ground and took them to the entrance where there were a couple of police. It was done with great dignity and no scene was made but after a couple had gone, there was no more trouble. It was very slick and evidently they had a well practised technique!

I don't think you have ever been into the Ball Room. It is quite impressive and when it is decorated with large flower arrangements and the candles are lit it is quite lovely. There are the large Luke Fildes portraits in pairs of King Edward VII and Queen Alexandria and George V and Queen Mary. There is a small portrait of Queen Victoria, and a small pair of George VI and Queen Elizabeth. There is incidentally a rather feeble reproduction of The Queen by James Gunn sent out by the Foreign Office recently, which hangs over the two grand chairs at the end of the Ball Room. HE wants to get a portrait that does her justice.

One elderly lady was quite rude to me and said "I had no business to come to New Zealand as an ADC engaged…it spoilt all the girls' fun!!! I told HE and he thought it very amusing. I think HE is mildly exasperated by Neil and his girl friends, as some weeks before he had a confrontation with an irate parent who thought his daughter was engaged to Neil only to discover this was not the case!

Next morning, after the dance, HE and the family went off to their beach house and I am here on my own. Yesterday afternoon I went for a long drive round Wellington, looking for places to paint. It is very exciting as I found a great deal of interesting subjects. In the evening a local, Ken Wright, gave a cocktail party in his house. Richard and Jane were there; there were several young English married couples who are in business, shipping or insurance. 14 of us went to the Jolly Frog which is about the only place in Wellington one can eat. I got back quite early but Neil brought a party back here, which stayed till after 4 am and you should see our room in the morning!

Section B - ADC to the Governor General, New Zealand 1959/1960

Extract of letter dated 18th September 1959.

This morning I went down to see Neil off at the airport. What a performance!

There were several groups of girls evidently distressed, biting back the tears, and no doubt hoping for 'the ring' at the last moment. Neil weaved his way round the departure hall kissing them, squeezing them and mopping back their tears and moving round to the next group. Suddenly he appeared outside, walking towards the plane, and there was an awful squawk from the girls, and he waved to them and was gone. One girl, Libby Todd, came up to me and said I was wearing the same suit as Blair, and thereupon burst into tears. Another girl turned to me streaming with tears and said "It's alright for you, separated but engaged, but I don't think I shall ever see Neil again." I said to Ken Wright who was standing there: "We must do something about this". Ken said "I have got some champagne left over from a recent wedding. We will tell them all to come to my house." Some minutes later about a party of ten turned up at Ken's house. We poured out the champagne, Ken and I went to the kitchen and fried some bacon and eggs.

Eventually with the help of the champagne, one by one the girls started talking….. "I think Neil behaved very badly with me… .he said he wanted to get engaged to me." "Oh the devil, he said the same to me." "You are not the only two, he said that to me too.." "Where was Neil last night? He told me he was having dinner at GH" "He was with me till 11pm" "Well damn it, he was with me from about 11.30 till after 3 am" Neil's movements the last week were discussed, each of the girls was furious that they had all been strung along. By the time Ken and I had cooked the breakfast they were all saying "I never want to see or think about that man again…" I think we had done them all a great kindness as each of them would have pined away, expecting something that would never happen and letters that would never come. They went home and in those brief moments, they got Neil out of their system…

Neil, married Judith Chalmers, of Come Dancing fame. He left the Navy and for many years worked for the BBC as a cricket commentator. I only once saw him again briefly and that was at a petrol station in the King's Road.

The Suez Canal [Suez Canal Company]

Cairo and the river Nile (L) and Ismalia (R). 1984" [Editor]

Government House, Wellington [NZ Government]

Lord Cobham at the Treaty of Waitangi Celebrations 1960. Philip on the right.
[NZ Government]

The Andrew Murray Church, Wellington painted by Philip [Family Collection]

South Island. Mount Tasman (L) and Mount Cook (R) [Editor]

South Island. Lake Te Anau. [Editor]

Philip and Fiona [Family Collection]

Flower arrangement painted by Philip [Family Collection]

Philip with his sister, Polly Bristol, and brother, Robert Erskine [Family Collection]

HM The Queen inspecting the Guard of Honour of the Scots Guards at Balmoral. 1967
[Family Collection]

The murial painted for HM The Queen Mother at Corndavon Lodge [Editor]

Philip with HRH Prince Philip, almost certainly at a Guards Association of Southern Africa Dinner. Philip was President of the Association for several years. [Family Collection]

Philip Painting in Tanganyika in 1954. [Family Collection]

One of Philip's South African paintings. [Family Collection]

Balmoral Forty years on. Reunion of the 1967 Guard: Andrew Parsons; David Drummond Moray and Kim Fraser. Philip was unable to attend. [D.D Moray]

40 FOR BREAKFAST

Extract of letter dated 27th September 1959.

Thursday evening we had a dinner party for the American Ambassador, Francis Russell. He is a charming man with rather an extrovert wife, who amused me. There was quite a drama during the evening as when the girls went back into the drawing room, they found the fireplace very hot and smoking; so hot one was not able to put one's hand on the marble. There was evidently something very wrong and bearing in mind this house is all wood, the fire brigade were called. Within less than five minutes they appeared, dressed to the teeth looking like space men. They were quick to realise that a fire had caught the wood surrounds behind the marble. After much heaving and pulling the whole mantlepiece was removed, making a frightful mess but necessary to avoid a serious fire. The party broke up at one o'clock….

As a complete contrast we had 40 of Kate's school friends to breakfast. They arrived at 7.30am. They are off on the island ferry later in the morning touring the South Island. Just imagine 40 Pollys to breakfast, I told the Naval ADC this was his party… right up his street, a chance to pick them young …!

Sunday evening…I am on my own, everybody is out. Time to ponder and reflect. This is an extraordinary job. I am acting a part. I don't feel I am part of the real world. Everything is provided from the moment I get up in the morning till I go to bed. I am surrounded by kindness. It's like being on the stage.

Last night I went to my first drawing class in the local Tech. There were about 14 of us and it lasted 2 hours; I did three drawings and I enjoyed it. There was a funny little man with a beard who was instructing us. The model was a middle-aged female with huge breasts, but not very attractive..….I think I can manage attending once a week. Everybody wants to see what I have been doing and my feeble work has been pinned on the drink cupboard door. It's amazing how many people suddenly want a drink in the ADC's room!

Section B - ADC to the Governor General, New Zealand 1959/1960

Extract of letter dated 22nd September 1959.

The new naval ADC, Murray Johnstone, has settled in. It's very much hit or miss, as this job is so dependent upon the people around one. We work as a team, share an office and we need to be compatible. My first impressions are very positive. He is a serious career naval officer - there is no harm in that - and has a very nice sense of humour and that's absolutely essential. It's not a criticism but he is far less tolerant of the inefficient way this place muddles along. Murray delivered a sharp reprimand to one of the idle footmen the other day, which I might add was quite justified and much needed, who then went along and complained to the Military Secretary. Murray was furious to be told footmen were far harder to replace than naval ADCs! One just has to laugh.

Extract of letter dated 1st October 1959.

Our routine continues. Last night I went with HE to a dinner at the United Services Club, all ex-servicemen. HE made a short but good speech which went down well. The evening turned into a heavy drinking session and there was much reminiscing and dirty stories. The previous evening there was a stag party here which HE evidently enjoys as Lady C is not here. There were seven old boys and they banged on till past one o'clock. We had two more similar parties. I find them quite interesting as one picks up the vibes of NZ, and what makes this country tick. Somehow when there is a mixed party everybody is on their best behaviour and far more restrained in their conversation. At these functions I think HE finds it a struggle to keep the conversation going, so he has a host of stories which he trots out every night. At the stag parties there is a much more interesting flow of conversation.

I think you will know there is a Labour Government in power here. It's not a criticism but an observation that this country is very socialistic. I think the experiences of the '30s and the Depression turned this country towards socialism, which has made New Zealand into a welfare state. It's a defensive mechanism for a small isolated state, but that's not the whole picture...I believe one has to go back to the First World War and Gallipoli, and then to the experiences of the Second. There developed in the Forces a great 'mucking in' spirit, a deep reliance on your mate…and when this is turned into politics you get a socialist cadre. There are no smart Regiments and no officer class as in the British Army. Their army is very small and relies on the territorial system of citizenship. Any form of status or class is anathema; a man is as good as his job…anyone who has acquired wealth is regarded with suspicion and there is something suspect about ambition. As a result those who do have either wealth or ambition, try and hide it. The irony of the situation is that HE is by nature in the opposite camp. Most of his lectures and speeches advocate free enterprise, but while they are listened to with respect, his audiences are deeply entrenched in the welfare state. I get the impression that Australia, in contrast, is more like America, a much more capitalist society. I pick up all these thoughts listening to the conversations at dinners when guests let their hair down.

Extract from a letter dated 10th October 1959.

Lord de la War and his wife have been staying, they are a very nice couple. They left on Wednesday. He is Chairman of the Royal Commonwealth Society. I was impressed by him. He is a dedicated man who gave up a respectable political career for this cause. He was a junior minister and then Post Master General in Eden's government. They live in Sussex not far from Granny. I think they enjoyed their stay; however, there was one evening when Tom and Rosemary Butler asked them to dinner. One of the guests was the Chancellor of Wellington University, who is a known communist, and he started deriding the Commonwealth Society; de la War was speechless with rage and returned back here extremely angry. I thought it was a good thing for him to know that those sort of people do exist here and he needed to meet them; it's no good preaching all the time to the converted. One realises there has only got to be one Governor General who fails, and it could make New Zealand into quite a tricky spot. The relationship between the two countries is always going to be sensitive; its fine at the moment but it would be a mistake to take anything for granted.

I have been doing some painting at last. The problem I find is to capture the brightness and the clarity of the light and get any sense of distance. The best light at dawn or dusk only lasts a few moments; the other problem is the wind which makes painting very difficult. There are an enormous number of subjects round Wellington to keep me fully happy for ages.

Extract from letter dated 11 October 1959.

Saturday, yesterday, I had the afternoon clear so I drove a considerable distance. I went up the Hutt Valley up into the high hills overlooking the Hutt river. I am completely smitten by the landscape, lovely clear lights and vivid colours and hard lines. I didn't paint, it was just a recce but I enjoyed my afternoon. Meanwhile the atmosphere in GH is as good as one could possibly expect; there are never any angry scenes and we all get on very well together. Murray has a great sense of humour and we all keep laughing. I think we are efficient and doing a good job. I like Lord C, he is direct, amusing and a most generous man. He has a quick brain and it is fun working here.

A VISIT TO AUCKLAND

Extract from letter dated 19th October 1959.

We have been busy. We had a lunch party on Thursday. Nio Marsh, the detective writer and eight other locals were asked. Then we had a small drink party for the medical fraternity in the evening for Sir David Campbell, the President of the Medical Council. He is a wizened old Scot, quite amusing and interesting. I was asked to dinner with Barry Blundell who owns the Evening News; it was a private do but there was quite a large gathering including the Australian High Commissioner, Sir John Collins and Lady Collins, the German and the Danish Ministers and their wives. I was quite amused to hear the conversations of the diplomatic world. I got back quite early and got involved talking to HE who wanted to know everything. I was given an introduction to the Blundells by Mike Bowater whose family do a lot of business with each other.

Friday was rather hectic. We were under pressure to get out a lot of invitations to a reception next week; Dave Fouhy always leaves these invitations too late. At the same time, I was on duty, trying to cope with a whole series of callers, meeting them and taking them in and out of HE's office and trying to keep their appointments to about thirty minutes each. The drill is that after thirty minutes I go into the office; HE gets up and shows his visitor to the door and I then show them out…. having got rid of one, I then take the next visitor in. If HE wants more time he asks for tea or coffee and then I know he wants an extra few minutes. Sometimes he walks the visitor out on to the lawn and they walk round the garden. It's a sort of shuttle service all morning.

Saturday morning early we flew up to Auckland from the new Wellington Airport. It was a very bumpy flight and I was glad to get to Auckland. The main engagement was to lay the foundation stone for the National Women's Hospital. It was a typical civic do with four speeches: the Chairman of the Board, the Minister of Health, the Prime Minister and then HE. We sat on a scaffolding dais in front of a large audience. The Bishop of Auckland read the blessing, but had to compete with the noise from the trotting race meeting going on next door; the very powerful microphone commentary completely drowned his holy words! Luckily it didn't coincide with HE's speech. We then drove to see a man called Stevenson. He has offered a large piece of ground to build a new Government House. The present building has problems. The University want the site and the building needs a great deal doing to it. So a completely new building is being considered. The piece of ground we were shown is on a peninsular jutting out into the sea, a really lovely place surrounded on three sides by water, but it's snag is that it's about 40 minutes outside the City, which may be considered too far.

After dinner I found myself talking to an old boy and told him I was considering going down to Central Otago in November to paint and see the country. He was very keen to tell me all about it. Without much ado he got into his car…… announcing that he was off to collect a map. About fifteen minutes later he returned, his eyes twinkling, saying "Would I like some gold?" I was a little amazed and said, "Of course, yes…" He pulled from his pocket two miniature gin bottles; one contained about a tenth of an ounce of small pellets of pure gold and the other some tiny flicks of gold in water. He explained how he had panned the gold from a river and then he showed me on a map where to go. He then wrote me a letter of introduction to a friend of his who lives in Alexandria, in Central Otago. He pinpointed on the map the various rivers I should go to. I am quite certain he was perfectly genuine. He had been a don at Cambridge and was a fellow of the Royal Society and a great expert on fungi. He told me where and how I could borrow the right equipment. I liked the idea of painting and panning gold.

After about half an hour of animated conversation, he said there is only one thing I want. I held my breath, dreading what was to follow. He said he liked my tie - would I give it to him? It was my Brigade of Guards tie and I had another. So I took it off and gave it to him. I had no option. He told me that next year he was attending the Royal Society bicentenary in London and he wanted to wear a tie like that. HE thought it was quite amusing that I gave my tie away for a pot of gold!

FALLING IN LOVE WITH NEW ZEALAND LANDSCAPE

2nd November 1959.

This weekend HE went to Blenheim with Murray for the centenary celebrations and only returns on Tuesday evening, away four days. I would have gone but I am doing the West Coat visit later in the month so it seemed only fair that Murray went. It suited me fine as I could get some painting done.

Saturday, the weather was perfect. I took my lunch and I headed off with no real idea where I was going, except in the general direction of going north. I went over what is commonly called, Picock Hill. It's spelt Piakiarika, which lies behind Paraparaumu. It is close to 900ft rising almost sheer from the coast. The view from the top is a 'Sight of the Gods'. I am spell bound by the crystal clear atmosphere which is totally unpolluted. I could see from Picton Sound to the snow covered mountains of the South Island. They might be more than fifty miles away but you feel you can touch them. I sat there absorbing the scene. I didn't go further and ate my lunch…and returned to GH in the late afternoon. Sunday, I went back to the same area and settled near a river but everything went wrong. I broke my turpentine bottle, I trod on a tube of paint, broke two brushes and got my car stuck. At one stage I was surrounded by small boys who asked me endless questions. I was going nearly frantic, but in the end I managed to paint quite a reasonable picture. Monday, after lunch as soon as I could get away, I was again on the road, painting. I had been invited sometime ago to go and paint on the Eastwick's farm. It is a short distance from Wellington. They showed me a fantastic place, right high up on the cliffs with a magnificent view looking right across three bays and with the South Island in the distance…. they were very hospitable and friendly. They had been great friends of Blair and Neil.

One could be quite lonely in GH when everybody is away. There is a certain amount to do in the mornings, office work and writing out invitations but in the afternoons I am completely clear and I can go out painting. It is simply wonderful to have no distractions and to concentrate on painting; there is no greater pleasure than getting out and exploring this highly paintable countryside. The other impression I have is that the country is vastly empty….. apart from the few towns so much is unspoilt. There is native bush untouched by man.

A VISIT TO THE WEST COAST OF THE SOUTH ISLAND

Extract from letter dated 13th November.

I am off tomorrow with HE for a three-day tour of the West Coast of the South Island. We fly to Westport and end up at Hokitika. We will have a very full programme going from one reception to another, then we motor the remainder of the way, ending up at Hokitika, the most southerly town on the West coast; it's an old gold mining centre.

On Thursday we had a big investiture. HE knighted six and gave out about 60 medals. The Investiture was conducted in the Ballroom with all the family and friends seated and watching. I had to put the medals on the cushion which Murray was holding; he turned and handed the cushion to HE. I was a bit worried that I might hand HE the wrong medal. Can you imagine the fuss if the wrong medal was given to the wrong person! In fact, it went very smoothly. Afterwards there was a bun-fight for an hour. We are doing another next week.

The most colourful figure was an old Maori chief who got an MBE. He was a splendid sight; he had a wonderful smile but hardly any teeth with bones in his ears and long back ribbons hanging down from the bones. He was dressed in a morning coat and had all his traditional Maori tikis (made of greenstone). I had a brief talk to him afterwards. There were several of Edmund Hillary's polar team who were receiving polar medals, which I am told are very rare.

HE when he is in full uniform looks a magnificent, imposing figure. One can quite understand why New Zealanders like an outside personality. He carries it off well. If ever there was an example of the 'Empire in action' it is at one of these investitures; the Queen's authority being delegated to her Governor General. It is a very special occasion.

Extract from letter dated 18th November 1959.

I have just got back from the West Coast tour this evening. I feel somewhat exhausted after three long and tiring days. One has to be on one's toes hundred percent of the time! It was full of interest and one had hardly a moment to relax.

John Purvis handed me a brief of about eight pages of everything that was going to happen in the next few days. I passed on the details to HE and he kept abreast of what was going to happen next...quite honestly it was mildly intimidating going off into the blue with only this brief as a guide.

Early Monday morning HE and I flew from Wellington to Blenheim, which lies at the north of the South Island, where we had a brief stay of less than an hour and then flew on to Westport, a short distance. We were met by the Mayor and civic leaders and taken off to a hotel where there was a large lunch party arranged, followed by a civic reception. HE arrived at the hall and inspected a guard of honour of local schoolboys. He then made his way to the dais. The mayor read a formal address of welcome and then HE replied. There were four other speakers…..it started to rain and all the rest of the formalities were hurried on. He walked round a great number of school children, talking to them here and there…finally we ended up at the hospital. The Management Board greeted him and the doctors and nurses were presented to him. He walked round the wards; there was a civic tea party. He was then whisked off to the Returned Servicemen's Club for a beer. Then there was a big dinner party given by an old boy called Skinner; he was deputy Prime Minister and very much appeared to be the King of the West Coast. He was not a bad chap, a socialist of course. He was a good host and HE evidently enjoyed himself.

Tuesday was much the same routine. We left Westport at 8.45 and had the most lovely drive up the Buller Gorge which is a very narrow gap in the hills. The road wound along the river edge with sheer cliffs on one side and the raging torrent of the Buller River on the other. In some places the road was carved out of solid rock. It could not have been a more lovely drive with the sun catching the wild bush. There were a few small settlements along the way and we stopped briefly at several schools. There was a reception at a small town called Reefton, and then we motored on to Greymouth. Greymouth is a coal-mining centre and a port. There was much the same routine as the previous day: a lunch party in the hotel given by the mayor followed by a civic reception, a loyal address and HE's reply and further speeches, a tea party at the hospital and a visit to the RSA Club, ending up with a dinner party and a dance given by the local jockey club. And to bed after midnight. I have never talked so much to officials and their wives. It was all very friendly and warm. This sort of intense activity HE is very good at doing; he can change from talking to school masters to the medical profession, to slightly sozzled RSA members …he is convincing with the racing fraternity and equally at home with the miners.

Wednesday was more or less the same again. We left Greymouth at 9.am and drove to a place called Kumara which was an old gold rush town, which is now virtually a ghost town. We were told less than 200 people lived there. One could clearly see where the buildings had once been; there was a small civic reception with the school children lined up. We were taken to see one of the only gold dredgers still in use and working. It was a very large contraption,

Heath Robinson at its best, and extremely noisy. We spent about an hour walking round it. It digs up a huge amount of gravel out of the river, which gets swirled round in drums 8ft across. The noise is unbelievable and the droppings are channelled and sprayed with water and eventually the very small pieces of gold are collected and then put through a series of filters; it collects about three to four breakfast cups of gold a day. In value about 2000 pounds sterling a day. We were told they expect to go on dredging for about another seven years. We were told the dredger cost £300,000 to build ten years ago. It was all very interesting. Then we drove on to Hokitika. We had the most glorious view of Mount Cook and Mount Tasman. It was very clear and I would have given my eyeteeth to stop and paint.

Hokitika is another ghost town, it has a huge wide main street with several magnificent buildings which would not look out of place in Birmingham, a vast Church, a huge civic hall and hotel and then at the end of the main street, nothing except bush scrub and a few derelict huts and the remains of many more. Once it was the largest town in New Zealand; when the gold rush was at its height in the 1880s there was a population of over 50,000 and harbour facilities for 70 ships. All that is left is the local farming community, which is about 9,000. It is in a lovely situation beneath the snow-clad Southern Alps. There was much the same routine as before: a large lunch given by the mayor, followed by a civic reception, the loyal address and HE's reply then a visit to the hospital and tea in the Town Hall. We left at 4.30 and were back at GH by 6.30. Only to be confronted by a dinner party of twelve...

I am left with a number of impressions. The West Coast is a very different part of the world...it is very isolated from the rest of the country, the climate is determined by its close proximity to the Southern Alps. It has a very high rainfall and the agricultural industry is very different...I would deduce that most people are struggling to make a livelihood there, and only survive on the support they get from the Central Government. They were genuinely pleased to see HE and I think a visit like this does a lot of good. But it was an exhausting three days.

THE ROUTINE OF GOVERNMENT HOUSE LIFE

Extract from letter dated 23rd November 1959.

We had an amusing half hour this morning; the Thai Ambassador came to present his credentials. It's rather like a little one act play. It starts off very formally with HE, who is dressed in a morning coat, positioned at the end of the Ballroom. He is flanked by the Military and Official secretaries and behind are the two ADCs. Meanwhile in the next room a small procession assembles. At the given moment, when all are in position, the butler throws the ballroom doors open; the Permanent Secretary of Foreign Affairs leads the new ambassador and his staff, all attired in very picturesque diplomatic uniforms with feathers and all, into the ballroom. The procession halts just short of where HE is standing. They both bow to each other. The Permanent Secretary announces the ambassador's name and he then makes a short formal speech. "I have the pleasure of presenting my predecessor's Letters of Recall and my Letters of Credence. I bring good wishes from my King (or President, whichever is the case). I hope to foster good relations between our two countries." HE then accepts the letters and makes a short formal reply. He then introduces his personal staff to the ambassador, and the ambassador introduces his staff to the Governor General. When this is complete, the rest of the proceedings become informal and the wives appear, drinks are served and eventually after about a quarter of an hour HE leaves the room and the ambassador and his staff depart.

There has been a succession of people coming to see HE. There was a naval lunch party as the Australian Admiral and the Captain of the Australian aircraft carrier HMAS Melbourne are here on a curtsey visit. There were lots of naval jokes; Murray was in his element…it was one of those occasions when the military ADC kept quiet. There was a huge thrash in the evening on the aircraft carrier which Murray attended.

I have done a number of drives in the Wellington area looking for suitable places to paint. I found a beautiful waterfall right up in the bush, which I am determined to return and paint. There is so much unspoilt natural forest of tree ferns which has a unique primeval character; one could almost imagine a dinosaur appearing. One is very aware that many farmers here are still living the pioneer life.

The longer I am in New Zealand the more I am falling in love with the country. I never expected to find so much beauty. The odd thing is that with one or two exceptions the local artists fail, in my humble opinion, to capture the magic of the New Zealand landscape. I suppose living and being brought up with it so much is taken for granted, and they have not suffered the pollution that we all known and hate. I have been getting all my equipment to take away tomorrow; I shall be armed with a number of bottles of whisky in case I need help. My car is full of boards. It's a most exciting expedition.

MY TOUR OF THE SOUTH ISLAND

Extract of a letter dated 3rd December 1959.

I have just arrived back from my tour of the South Island, feeling quite exhausted; it was the greatest fun. I covered 1400 miles in eight days. As it is a part of the world you know, I will describe in some detail where I went.

I left on Monday evening and took my car on the night ferry to Lyttleton. I thought I should make my way immediately to Queenstown, a 350-mile drive, and not linger on the way, although there were some sensational places and breath-taking views of the Southern Alps, Mount Cook and the lakes of Central Otago. I found a very reasonably priced hotel on a lakeside and spent three nights there. Each day I rose early and went out painting. I had a rough idea what I wanted to do. I found a spot on the edge of Lake Hawea, the picture turned out quite well and another on the banks of the Clutha River. I was very fortunate with the weather, it was perfect. Having come all this way I thought I must go through to Milford Sound. On Friday I drove to a spot on Lake Te Anau and painted on the way and found a perfectly acceptable small hotel where I stayed the night. Next morning I drove through to Milford, going up the Holliford Valley where I stopped and painted, then on through the Homer tunnel into Milford Sound. It is the most dramatic country, but so much depends on the weather. I was lucky and had wonderful clear views, but as it was late in the afternoon I didn't paint and found a motel where I stayed. Next morning, after a thunder storm it was a complete wash out.

There was no point hanging round in those conditions so I made my way back to Lake Te Anau and spent a couple hours painting in the Eglington Valley. Next morning I motored round Lake Manapouri. Although very scenic, the problem was that there was a great deal of thick bush round the lake and it was very difficult to find a good spot. It was somewhat disappointing. I decided to drive on. I drove through Lumsden, Gore, Balclutha and Dunedin and finally spent the night at Omaru in a small hotel. Next morning, Tuesday, I wanted to be in Christchurch by the late afternoon. I passed a signpost to Coldstream, I stopped at a garage and rang the Studholmes, as I thought Imogene might still be there. I was told she was now at Mount Peel with the Aclands *[cousins of John Acland who was serving in the Scots Guards]*. I rang her there and she very kindly asked me to lunch. It's all fairly remote country and there is hardly a sign of a soul for miles as you can well understand, mile after mile of dirt roads and it was a question of guess work trying to find Mount Peel. I passed a man on the side of the road cutting grass, so I stopped and asked him if I was going in the right direction for Mount Peel? He replied I was. We had a few words and then he said could he see the paintings in the back of my car? We were still on the side of the road so I took them out and stood them against the car…explaining they were far from finished. I said I had been told to make contact with a local artist, Austin Deans. "Well, you have met him now! I am Austin Deans…" We had an animated conversation and I was very late for lunch. It was a complete fluke or a one in a million chance to meet him by accident.

I had a very pleasant lunch with the Aclands and Imogene; she seems very happy and much more relaxed. She told me she has got a flat in Christchurch and wants to settle permanently there. The Deans live almost next door to Mount Peel. I motored on to Christchurch and then caught the evening ferry at Lyttleton and arrived back here this morning.

CHRISTMAS FESTIVITIES AND A DANCE

Extract from letter on Boxing Day 1959.

Yesterday, Christmas. I thought so much about you and so wished we could have been together. We went to the midnight service at the Parish Church at the end of the drive. It was a very nice service…. We walked back up the hill to GH and talked for hours and then Murray, Julie and I distributed the children's stockings. We used the stockings Mother made for me sometime ago as nobody else had really good large stockings; by 7o'clock the house was in uproar! All six children were wildly excited and paper was strewn the length of GH. By 10.45 we all went to the Cathedral, all dressed up with HE in a morning coat and Murray and I in uniform. HE read both lessons. There was a large family lunch party, then we played tennis and, as it was a lovely day for a change, some of us went to swim in Wellington Bay. There was a small dinner party in the evening with the American Ambassador and Admiral Villiers and their families. It was a highly amusing party and HE was in great form. He was wearing a green bow tie, which lit up on a battery.

Nicky, the youngest boy had been given a rocket which, when filled with water and air rocketed up into the sky. It was suggested if the water was substituted for gin the rocket would go further. HE said it would and the American Ambassador said it wouldn't. Bets were laid, the rocket was filled with high-octane gin and we all went out on the lawn for the test to take place. The rocket was fired and went twice as far with gin inside it! There were jokes about Cape Canaveral. After dinner we played ballroom cricket. The Cobham family against the rest. We used a small bat and a soft ball and every run counted for ten. All the fielders were seated on chairs. The top scorer was the American Ambassador's wife. The game dissolved into chaos but everybody enjoyed it. We listened to The Queen's speech at dinner on an old wireless and then we all had a go at writing HE's New Year speech, which is being recorded tomorrow. It was suggested by someone he might get inspiration from inside one of the crackers so we all read out the messages, but I don't think it helped.

My main feeling during all the fun was how sad not being together with you. Nevertheless, the Cobham family did their utmost to make one happy and they gave us the most generous and wonderful presents. They are a very kind and sweet family and I do feel very fortunate doing this job with them. A contemporary of mine in the Regiment was with the Slims in Australia and got sent home for not being up to the job. Apparently, Lady Slim eats up ADCs like peanuts and after any event she lines them up for post mortems and the procedure is known as Woomera Rocket Range…so I count myself lucky!

Nearly everything is closed down in Wellington till well past the New Year. Everybody has either gone away or is going away. They are all off to their 'batch'. As you know the term 'batch' covers almost everything from a very smart beach house on the coast, to a simple hut on the side of a mountain; almost everybody has a 'batch'! The Cobhams are off to their beach house with the whole family until mid-January. Murray is off to Lake Taupo to fish and chase the female fraternity up there. I can amuse myself without any difficulty and I am quite happy to remain here on duty and get some painting done in the afternoons. It is quite expensive staying away and there is no point at the moment. I am planning a long trip back to my favourite haunts in the South Island, sometime in the New Year.

I was quite pleased I sold one of my rather indifferent paintings to a married couple for ten pounds. I am beginning to get into production and it makes sense if I can sell the odd one. I will keep the best – don't worry! The framing shop has an art gallery attached and has asked me to let them have a few paintings for an exhibition later next year. I think that sounds rather fun.

Day after Boxing Day. We had a huge party for the staff last night. Murray and I washed up and put everything away. I spent the day at the beach with Richard and Jane. Now the house is empty.

NEW ARRIVALS AND THE GARDEN PARTY INVITATIONS

Extract from letter dated 7th January 1960.

I went out to dinner on Sunday with Admiral Villiers. He is a great charmer and they are a very nice family. They are extremely kind and when one is here on one's own it makes a great difference to get out of GH to see a friendly family. for an odd meal. He is the New Zealand Chief of the Naval Staff and leaves in March and is being replaced by a NZ officer. Apparently there has been an awful row about this. Until now the appointment has been filled by a British naval officer; however, the Labour Defence Minister made a series of statements saying in future all three service chiefs of staff would be New

Zealanders. This put the government in an awkward position because they knew they had no one suitable. In the end they had to promote someone to the rank of Admiral just in order to save face. The Lords of the Admiralty are furious. The reason behind it is quite clear. Australia has an Australian Admiral and New Zealand has to keep pace with Australia, so New Zealand must have her own Admiral. It was bound to come sooner or later. This is just another example of the sensitive relationship between Britain and New Zealand. Taking the same issue a step further, sooner or later the same argument will be applied to finding Governor Generals. Australia will lead, New Zealand will follow. But as long as a distinguished and popular person fills the appointment of Governor General, the issue will lie dormant.

My desk is a complete mass of paper. We sent out 4000 invitations for the Wellington garden party; replies are coming in and now we are in the process of sending out another 4000 invitations for the Auckland garden party.

I feel so fortunate having my painting as an interest as it keeps me sane! The beauty of this country is beyond compare and the challenges it offers to an artist are frustrating. It's like chasing the end of a rainbow as, at times one gets so near, yet one knows one's ability is miles away from capturing a satisfactory result. Wellington has two moods…one is pure perfection with wonderful crystal clear days; the other is quite the opposite, stormy, windy, tempestuous days throwing up all the anger that comes across the Tasman Sea. In pursuing Mother Nature, one finds she is a very elusive lady!

A DAY'S RACING AT TRENTHAM

Extract of letter dated 16th January 1960.

I never finished my last letter. We were completely snowed under with paper work; 8000 invitations are quite enough to kill one! Then in the evening Murray and I went to see a film called 'Some like it Hot' with Marilyn Munroe. Light hearted nonsense but quite entertaining and anything to take one's mind off invitations!

Yesterday I went to Trentham Races with HE and Lady C, Julie Wilding and old Dave Fouhy. It struck me that Trentham is really more like Goodwood than any other course I know. HE hates racing: he hates the awful deafening gabble of the racing commentary. He doesn't like or understand horses and has no interest in their breeding and has little in common with the racing fraternity. Lady C on the other hand is quite amused. Julie, of course, knows the racing world well and most of the owners, and old Dave Fouhy is in his element on the racecourse. I had a very amusing day but I feel a bit of a fool - wandering round in a dark suit and bowler hat which couldn't be more out of place. The rules are that the ADC wears the same order of dress as HE and if he goes in a dark suit and bowler hat, I have to do the same. HE's presence is quite formal. We arrived in the new Rolls, its first outing, in time for the second race and were taken by the President of the Meeting to the President's Box. The band played 'God save the Queen' and then we watched the second race. We were then taken to lunch with the members. There was a huge display of food on tables as far as you could see. All perfectly arranged. It was a stand-up meal. All the Diplomatic Corps were there but it was a somewhat stiff affair. It was no good pretending it was something HE enjoyed. For the big race, the Wellington Cup, we were taken to the Stewards' Stand and watched it from there, after which HE presented the cup and made a short speech, which went down well. We watched one further race and then left.

HE returned to GH last Wednesday when we had a very hectic day. The Indian High Commissioner presented his letters of credence. Then there was last minute panic, the Italian ambassador, who calls himself The Duke of Regina, should have followed but at the last moment he rang GH to say he had mislaid his letters! He only discovered it at the last moment. I thought it was killingly funny but HE was not amused! I suggested he mixed them up with his spaghetti! The Venezuelan ambassador followed. I am rather surprised that New Zealand makes a fuss about Venezuela but I was told that is where this country gets its oil.

Friday evening, HE had dinner here; they came back from their beach house in the afternoon. There was no party but we played bridge all night. He adores his bridge; he plays with Lady C against Murray and myself. She is a weak player; he is very good and Murray and I are just about average so it's quite balanced. As you know I have played bridge since I was a small boy but hardly in recent years; I feel very rusty. The honours at the end of the evening were divided almost equally. What I do find a little disconcerting is next morning's post mortem when HE wants to show me how I could have made a slam. Once a hand is over, I forget it completely. Just imagine trying to remember one hand out of, say, twelve the night before. HE can not only remember what he had in his hand but also remember what I had. There is a re-play on the breakfast table. I feel very foolish; I cannot remember anything!

THE MALAYASIAN PRIME MINISTER'S VISIT

Extract from letter dated 20th January 1960.

After a long period of non-activity life at GH has gone to the opposite extreme. The last 24 hours has witnessed some very colourful and quite spectacular scenes.

The Malaysian Prime Minister arrived yesterday afternoon on a State Visit with his wife (who looked like one of the girls I once met in Aladdin's Cave in Cairo). A huge figure with an utterly blank expression on her face, hardly surprising as we were told she had had fourteen children! On the other hand her daughter in law, who acted as her lady in waiting was very pretty wearing the most gorgeous silk dress covered in lovely jewellery. They all arrived in a procession, which would only have been surpassed by a Presidential drive down 5th Avenue. Six of the biggest Ford cars in NZ made their way slowly up the drive. In the rear five cars were the Prime Minister's staff, Press Secretaries, aides of one sort or another, packed like sardines, and endless other staff, excellent looking men, who transpired to be baggage men (no doubt doubling as security!). There were a battery of cameramen and the whole press corps was assembled outside GH. Inside, waiting was HE, in morning coat, and Lady C in a long dress and all the staff in 'best bib and tucker' and the whole cabinet lined up like a chorus line… There were all sorts of funny little men running round, who added to the confusion.

The scene that followed was pure theatre. It could have been a Royal Premier. There were the blinding flashes of scores of cameramen. All jostling each other. The introductions were more like a rugby match. Low on dignity but strong on colour. Nobody knew who anybody was. Out of this confusion somehow Murray and I were told by the Military Secretary to sort the crowd out into two parties; those required to stay and those who we wanted to go. It was most difficult as every politician wanted to be photographed, either inside or outside GH. We hadn't a clue who half the characters were. Eventually, we managed to get some semblance of order and extracted the few who were to stay and we closed the doors. It was all fairly brutal! Looking back on it, I was amazed that it was not better organised. This is billed to be a very important political event, a State Visit; it was a complete shambles.

We had a very sticky dinner party in the evening, just the Malayans and us. The two ladies on HE's right and left couldn't speak a word of English. There was one amusing moment, which broke the tension, when the Malaysian Prime Minister said to Lady C how much he had enjoyed the hot springs near Lake Taupo; the table convulsed in laughter as we all knew what had happened to Murray a few days before when he got into the hot springs with a bottle of champagne and a host of pretty girls… and it was explained to the PM the dangers of the hot springs. Rather silly but it was a difficult dinner. HE went on telling stories which I don't think were understood by our visitors but anything was better than endless silences.

This morning, the Malaysian party have been at Trentham for the annual yearling sales and various other engagements, which have not concerned me. There is a big dinner party tonight for 24, the Cabinet and senior nobs…..

I get driven mad by the endless changing of plans. It is quite obvious their programme has not been thought out and it is changed every day. In this job you keep smiling, and somehow everything must be a pleasure, even if one is driven nearly mad.

Extract from letter dated 25th January 1960.

I haven't written for three days as we have been flat out running round after the Malaysians. Murray and I spend a great deal of time hanging round, a plan is made and then altered and re-altered and then changed again, and nobody knows what is happening next. I cannot think of greater confusion.

Section B - ADC to the Governor General, New Zealand 1959/1960

It's certainly not the way to have a so-called 'State Visit'. In fact when the Malaysians left on Friday we were not at GH to see them off.

We had a big pompous white tie dinner party for them on Wednesday evening. The Malaysian Prime Minister wore his native dress and his ladies looked very pretty in their silk dresses. In contrast our team looked very dull; Nash, the NZ Prime Minister, and Holyoke the Leader of the Opposition, and a few senior souls. The table looked lovely with a mass of gold plate in the middle (belonging to HE) and huge candlesticks with orange candles and orange silk tablemats. There was no other source of light except from the candles; it made a fantastic setting, and a sight I will never forget.

The following day I was included in the State lunch given by the Malaysian Prime Minister in the Parliament buildings for 300. The lunch itself was very ordinary, except for the scale of the party. The speeches were endless, Nash spoke for 35 minutes, Holyoake followed and spoke for 30 minutes, the minister of Maori Affairs for 15 minutes so by the time the Malaysian PM, the Tunku, got to his feet we were suffering. In fact he was very amusing, spoke very well and shortly, but it dragged on till past 4 o'clock.

The last evening the Malaysian party were here, we were at rather a loose end to know how to amuse them. A dinner party had been arranged and then cancelled. We had had them already once by themselves so we didn't want to have a repeat. In the end HE decided to take them to the beach house and give them dinner there, cooked by Lady C and us! The Tunku was thrilled out of his mind as he drove the new Rolls Royce to the beach house, doing between 80 and 100 mph most of the way, while Murray, his ADC and I followed in another car trying to keep up. The evening was an unparalleled success. They all relaxed and what might have been a very dull evening became a most amusing party. After dinner HE produced a question book, which had questions and answers on every subject under the sun. Our guests thoroughly enjoyed this. We got them very merry despite them being Moslems, and the Tunku was very funny, imitating and taking off Mr Nash and the politicians he had met. They 'all let their hair down' and it was great fun. HE and the Tunku are both about the same age and had many things in common; both had been to Cambridge, although not together, but shortly after each other. They both had been tutored by many of the same dons; both had read law; both liked fast cars and no doubt, when younger fast girls!

Friday morning a film unit took elaborate shots of all of us in groups and in various positions. I think it was mainly for the Malaysian public. The final scene before they departed was the exchange of gifts. The Tunku produced a huge box of presents which he gave to all the important personages; alas the ADCs were not included, not that we expected anything. They were most magnificent gifts. He gave HE a box containing an eight piece silver tea set. I think it was native craftsmanship and to Lady C a huge roll of silk. HE, I think, felt a little embarrassed not having something of equal value to give; anyway nothing was given in return which I thought was a mistake. On reflection, I wonder if it was realised that gifts were going to be exchanged. The planning of the visit was all very poorly organised from start to finish, but it didn't in any way diminish the good will that had developed between us all.

Friday evening, we all went to see Sir Donald Wolfit's production of Shakespeare; it was a Shakespeare review, the only actors being Sir Donald and his wife. It was quite well done. Saturday, we had no rest. HE's uncle Richard Lyttleton and his wife came to stay and we had a big dinner party of 22 in the evening. It was a bit stiff and sticky; I think we were all rather tired, not in our best form and for me, the evening dragged. Sunday, we all went to the Cathedral; it's always a very nice service. I have grown to love Wellington Cathedral and I find worship is a great comfort in our long separation. We sang the 'The Lord's my Shepherd' which brought tears to my eyes. Then Sir Donald Wolfit and his wife came to lunch. They are a most amusing couple and kept us laughing the whole meal. He looks like nothing on earth, long hair, huge eyes and an attractive voice and a continuous flow of stories.

This evening the family arrived back in time for dinner. It was not until after dinner did we discover what had happened out at the beach house earlier in the day. The old uncle, Richard Lyttleton, went swimming and got carried out by the sharp undertow of the current and was very pushed to get back to the shore. Lady C saw what had happened and went to his rescue and she also got into difficulties. HE was some distance away but saw what was happening and called three strong youths to get them back. The two were exhausted and frightened but otherwise nothing else. It was very lucky and a lesson for others. Actually, the beach there is no more dangerous than Jersey but the golden rule is not to go out above one's waist, as at certain times the tide is very strong and sucks one out quickly. Both were well with no ill effects, but I dread to think what might have happened. I have tried to give you all the news and as you will see we have been very busy.

In the olden days at courts there was a character called the court jester... whose job it was to amuse people and break the tension at social events. I am more and more clear that my role as ADC is much the same ...at times play the fool, and prompt HE to tell the next story and generally keep everything on a light note.

THE GARDEN PARTY AT GH

Extract from letter dated 31st January 1960.

Thursday we had the dreaded Garden party. I say dreaded as it's been the centre of nearly two months work. It poured with rain non-stop all the morning; it simply couldn't have been worse. Then at midday the weather changed and by a miracle of the Gods the sun came out and it was just perfect, but, as the last guests were leaving, the heavens opened again. I think we had about 3500, there may have been a few more. It proved to be a scrum and I don't think people could circulate much.

I was kept very busy. We were divided up into two teams. Murray, Dave Fouhy and an Honorary ADC with HE. Julie, Jock Harrison, the Military Secretary, and myself with Lady C. We worked as a team, picking people out from the crowd and presenting them. One had to work fast, finding out their names and a little about them so Lady C could make a few sensible remarks to them. Of course, all Wellington was there. I got hold of Richard and Jane and took them up to Lady C. I was impressed how many were in morning coats. The event was regarded as a success. I think it gave everybody a chance to see HE and Lady C.

One of the jobs I did yesterday was to go and see an old lady called Mrs Seddon, she keeps asking to see my paintings, and asks me to take them round to show her. I have made several excuses but as we are going to be away for two months I would try and fit it in. I went round for half an hour and I think she was pleased; her father in law was the famous New Zealand Prime Minister

Richard Sadden; you may have heard of him since he was the first Prime Minister after New Zealand gained Dominion status, and remained Prime Minister for many years.

THE MOVE TO AUCKLAND AND THE TREATY OF WHAITANGI CELEBRATIONS

Extract from letter dated 6th February 1960.

I have been on the move almost continuously for the last six days. The move to Auckland went smoothly. I loved the chance of seeing new country and as I was on my own I could take my time.

The Auckland Government House is much smaller than that at Wellington. I have been told this is the last year it will be used by the Governor General and then it will be handed over to Auckland University. The story is they want to expand into the grounds, not that the garden is very large, but it is in a central position in the city centre. The building itself is much smaller; we have got a small office by the door that gets cluttered up every delivery and there is hardly any room to work. Murray and I have a small hut in the garden about eighty yards from the main entrance. It's perfectly adequate for a few weeks. The general impression is that we are camping there.

I met up with everybody who had come his or her different ways to Auckland. We had hardly time to get settled when we flew up the following morning to the Bay of Islands. It was quite an experience; we flew up in an old Sunderland flying boat. I have never been in one before. It is very heavy and noisy and takes a great deal of distance to take off on water. She flies very slowly. When we landed in the Bay of Islands the entire New Zealand fleet were anchored in the Bay. It was an amazing sight. What should have happened was a small boat should have come alongside and taken our party off, but nothing happened and we sat there bobbing around on the sea for three quarters of an hour, being completely ignored by one and all! HE was not amused! The various attempts to attract attention went unheeded. In the end a boat did come and take us to the shore. Apparently the Admiral was doing his inspection of the fleet and nobody was thinking of anything else. Sometime later in the afternoon Admiral Villers came to see HE and apologised…I think Murray had rather fun telling the senior officers how furious HE was!

The Treaty of Whaitangi was made between the Maori people and the English Settlers in the name of Queen Victoria. The terms of the Treaty are regarded as a special step in the relationship between the two peoples of New Zealand. The annual celebrations are a reminder to everybody that this special relationship remains honoured.

Next morning, the weather was perfect and it was a lovely setting with the whole New Zealand fleet in the Bay, dressed overall. All the service personnel were in their best. There was an atmosphere of ceremonial expectation, slightly like at home on the day of the Queen's Birthday Parade. HE was dressed in full ceremonial white and cock feathers and was due to inspect a guard of honour, but before doing so he had to accept the Maori challenge. A Maori warrior dressed in full splendour advanced towards him and threw down a stick, which HE had to pick up, but in so doing there was a rip in his very tight trousers and His Imperial Excellency's bottom was exposed! There was nothing that could be done, as he was just about to inspect the Guard of Honour and then stand on a podium to address the multitude. The only defensive action that could be taken was for the two ADCs to keep close and shield his problem. HE gets full credit; he didn't blink or flinch and carried on as if nothing had happened. It was only when we got back to the Treaty House was HE able to change.

As you can imagine there were a series of speeches. The Prime Minister and several Maori leaders spoke for hours and then there was a reception in the Treaty House.

The following morning we had a delightful day with the Villiers family on the Admiral's barge…we toured the Bay of Islands and found a dream place to have lunch and then we tried to shoot wild goats but failed. Next day, yesterday, we flew back to Auckland. We have a very full programme ahead of us for the next few weeks.

Lord Cobham's speech at the 120th anniversary of the signing of the Treaty of Waitangi, February 1960.

"Mr Prime Minister, Your Excellency, Hon Ministers and Distinguished guests Ladies and Gentleman.

This is the most important of all days in the history of New Zealand, for it was the day on which, one hundred and twenty years ago, the pattern was set, and the new tapestry was planned, in which light threads and dark ones were to be interwoven to form the completed study of a new Nation.

Against the wide background of time, in relation to the world's history, it is true to say that the tapestry is only just begun The intervening years have not been easy ones for the Maori people. They have had to try to adjust themselves in only just over a hundred years to a way of life that it took western men two thousand years to achieve.

In an age when we all are facing social problems of great complexity to which we are still trying to find solutions, particularly in the crowded and often unhealthy atmosphere of great cities, it is perhaps hardly surprising to find that some young people find it difficult to attune their lives to modern social and industrial conditions. Their history is of a seafaring people; in other words they were and are an open-air and pastoral people – and they have suddenly found themselves translated into an age of science and machine.

Europeans are themselves only too sadly aware of the effects of materialism upon their own religious beliefs towards the close of the last century. Many of our old disciplines have been sacrificed on the altars of the new tolerance, and the so-called 'progressive thinking'. It is hard to lead in an age wherein so many people deem it their inalienable right to act or think as they please, wherein knowledge and experience are shrugged off as outworn and old-fashioned commodities. A century ago the family unit was the one wherein children learnt self-control and the ideal of future service, and the schools merely reflected and continued that educational process. A century ago the wise Maori Elders exercised that same discipline in their communities. Now both have been weakened and, having sown the wind, we must see to it that we don't reap the whirlwind.

Today I am calling on the Maori people to do all in their power to encourage and foster leadership among their own folk. Only through the closest possible co-operation between the leaders of both races in New Zealand, can the best use be made of the splendid material which must be for ever more closely woven to make it lasting and strong. Each has its own special and vital contribution to make towards this end. In war it proved unbreakable and it must be unbreakable in peacetime.

If this real integration takes place, not only will New Zealand become immeasurably happier and more prosperous, but she will also have made a significant contribution towards solving the racial difficulties of others.

Today, New Zealand Day, is the one from which the nationhood of this country stems. It is one which is coming to receive greater recognition as the years roll by. Fresh resolutions by both Maoris and Europeans are needed, if Captain Hobson's century old dream is to become that dimly-discerned reality towards which the whole world is striving. It is right that this day of re-dedication should always be faithfully preserved."

ROUTINE IN AUCKLAND

Extract from letter 12th February 1960.

Our life in Auckland has rather a different rhythm. I think it's partly because we are all camping, living a rather temporary existence. Also, there is a considerable difference between Wellington and Auckland. Wellington is made up of civil servants, parliamentarians and professional people; of course there are exceptions. Auckland has a very active business community and is the only part of New Zealand that has any industrial area with a wide range of light industries. Its heartbeat is closer to Sydney than Wellington. It is clearly a more prosperous city. The City Council is made up of rather quarrelsome businessmen. We had our first dinner party for the City Council two evenings ago. Dave Fouhy told us it was going to be very sticky as there were several legal battles flying round…nobody was speaking to anyone!

It was an extremely muggy evening. We were all seated on the veranda and HE was holding forth, as nobody was making any effort to talk; the silence was painful. Anyway, HE held his glass up and asked me to fill it. I was standing behind him; I held the jug of dry martini at arm's length, poured out what I thought was a full glass but I had misjudged the distance and poured the whole drink down the sleeve of his coat. The entire party saw it happen; HE said nothing, then lowered his arm and shook his sleeve and the liquid flowed out. In a quiet aside he said "That what I have to put up with from my staff!' Suddenly the tension was broken and all the councillors started to laugh. It was almost slapstick comedy but it worked the trick…and from that moment on, the party was a roaring success. We plied them with as much drink as they would consume and that was considerable. By the end of the evening they were walking down the drive arm in arm…stoned out of their minds, seemingly the best of pals. No doubt they would be hammering each other next morning in the Council Chamber, but for a moment we did our job by giving them a very good party and they all thought the world of HE. It was another example of the ADC's role, playing the court jester. I broke the tension, albeit by accident…but a stiff pompous party would have served no good. HE was excellent at sensing the moment and playing along with it, and later he said how well the home team had done.

Most mornings HE goes out on some visit taking either Murray or myself. There have been a stream of small dinner parties and receptions, somehow we take them in our stride and the pace is quite fast. However, the other day there was a bit of a hiccup. The footmen were being quite idle and slow and Murray got a move on them with a few sharp words, which might have been suitable for the quarterdeck, but they went off sulking to Jock Harrison. Instead of Jock blasting them as they deserved, he sent for us and we were told footmen were far harder to get than ADCs! Later we made a joke of it and told HE who was entirely on our side!

Section B - ADC to the Governor General, New Zealand 1959/1960

Extract of letter dated 19th February 1960.

Our life continues at quite a fast pace. Yesterday the garden party went off very well. The weather was perfect. It was all very friendly and colourful. It took much the same form as at the earlier party in Wellington. I think we were better organised in the sense that we made a plan to circulate better; HE and his team went round clockwise; Lady C and her team, including myself, went round anti-clockwise and we met in the middle and returned to the House.

Earlier this morning there was quite an amusing situation. I was woken at about 3am in the morning by one of the telephone operators. "You must take this telegram to His Excellency" "Cannot it wait till the morning?" I protested. No, he was quite emphatic that HE must receive the telegram immediately. Now I had no idea of the geography of the rooms upstairs in Government House. I had no reason previously to go there. Ignorance was no excuse so I made my way into the house, which had to be unlocked. The whole was pitch dark, I went up the stairs, and I stopped and listened. I could hear HE snoring so I turned left, I followed the sound of his snoring. I opened his bedroom door and could faintly see his body lying there. "Sir, I have a telegram you must read." "Cannot it wait for the morning?" "No, sir, I am afraid I am instructed to give it to you to read now." "Oh hell!' he said trying to turn on the light, "What's all this nonsense about..." He went on tearing open the envelope. He heaved a sigh grunting, "The Queen has had a son!" There were a few more grunts. I retreated and went back to bed. At 8 o'clock a press statement was released to say that Their Excellencies were delighted to receive news from Buckingham Palace that Her Majesty had had a son. I fielded questions all the morning "What was His Excellency's reaction to the news?" "Absolutely delighted, we are all absolutely delighted!"

The child grew up to be Prince Andrew, the Duke of York.

One of the features of our life in Auckland is the continual arrival of presents. I find it quite difficult to make up my mind about the situation. Father, as Governor in Jersey, had a firm rule 'no presents'. Of course, he would accept a small box of chocolates when someone came to dinner or the odd bottle of wine, but anything of any substance was returned with a polite letter. He was most anxious not to be seen exploiting the goodwill of the island. When he left, again he made it known he would only accept nominal presents. However, in Auckland the presents flowed in at an embarrassing rate… Boxes of underclothes for the staff, and God knows what for the girls! I am afraid there was no reluctance on anyone's part about accepting these gifts. It pricked my conscious but apparently this happened every year and it was accepted as the norm. I do concede it reflected goodwill and it was felt churlish not to accept them.

Extract from letter dated 23rd February 1960.

In my earlier letters I listed many of the various people who came through the doors of Government House but here the pressure is far greater…There is a nurses' reception one evening, a group of students another and there is a reception for service personnel, mainly the Navy. Also, groups of businessmen at each dinner party and so on.

I am beginning to miss Wellington. It was so easy to drive out of Wellington and very quickly get into real country. The rugged landscape round Wellington has great appeal to me and I found it easy to find endless places to paint. But Auckland has a large suburban area and one has to drive miles before one can find open unspoilt country. The weather is milder and muggy which I don't enjoy and I don't know my way around here, nor do I get the chance to explore as we are kept busy.

DRAMA ON LAKE TONGARIRO

Extract from letter dated 28th February 1960.

I feel I am writing the same, again and again, but the reality is that we are doing a very concentrated programme, and our routine is very repetitive. I rather enjoyed last weekend. It was decided that HE and Lady C needed a break and a short visit to Taupo was planned. I was sent down on Thursday to report on the fishing as it made a big difference to the equipment they took, depending on where they are advised to fish. There were quite a number of alternatives, but depending on a number of factors some places were much better than others. I drove down to stay with Harold Hickling and next morning went and did a recce. I went to the fishing shop, a short distance and asked where the fish were being caught. Old Hickling also had a view and I went to a couple of other places and then telephoned HE and gave him a summary of what I had discovered. It was decided that I would stay there and act as messenger boy…while HE and Lady C fished. What I didn't know was that Old Hickling had lived for some time after the war near Stellenbosch and according to HE, he went through his wife's money and fled to NZ! Somewhere along the line he picked up Mrs Anstruther. However, they were very kind to me, but they tended to grumble that HE didn't reciprocate their hospitality. I tried to make a joke of it and told him to marry Mrs Anstruther! I volunteered to be the best man… play the court jester!

There was quite a drama on Sunday. I will explain. The weather was perfect, not a cloud in the sky. It was decided that Lady C, with the Admiral, Faran Grace, who was the Maori boatman and myself would go to the far side of Lake Tongariro, where we would fish. Everything went smoothly. We drove and collected Faran Grace and made our way in a landrover across country to where the boat was moored. The lake is long and thin curving round the base of Mount Tongariro, I think about eight or ten miles in length and about a thousand yards wide. We had no difficulty making our way across the lake; it was perfectly calm like a millpond. We found a small bay where some small mountain stream flowed into the lake and there we pottered all the morning. Lady C and Faran Grace fished from the boat and I rather feebly attempted from the shore. We had a delicious lunch and we pottered on till about 4, when we thought we should start making our way back. But what none of us had noticed was that out in the open lake the water had become very choppy and a strong wind was blowing. It was generally decided that we would not risk the crossing but wait till the wind dropped. The wind did not drop and the conditions got worse. The afternoon turned to evening and soon it was dark. We were still the far side of the lake. Incidentally, I have to say there was no way round on the ground. It was too sheer and rugged. Faran Grace was for staying put; the Admiral was for making the crossing. It was decided to go out from our sheltered bay and judge the conditions when we got into the open lake. Faran Grace was against making the crossing, he said he knew the lake from childhood and it wasn't worth taking the risk. The Admiral said he knew how to get us back and that he wasn't going to be told anything by the Maori boatman. The crossing was only about a thousand yards but it was an extremely unpleasant experience. I know Lady C was frightened out of her wits. We were positioned at the back of the boat and in order to avoid being thrown around we linked arms and held ourselves tight against the side of the boat. Give the Admiral his due, he did manage to get us back, but there was a 'Red Alert out' as we were reported missing. There was a large reception group waiting and HE was distinctly worried and angry.

It just shows how dangerous those lakes can be and how quickly they can turn nasty, every year there are tragedies in that part of the world. We should never have risked the crossing back. It was the general opinion we were very lucky not to have drowned.

Extract of letter dated 4th March 1960.

The subject of South Africa keeps cropping up at dinner parties. It usually starts with a question like. "What does His Excellency think about South Africa?" HE is remarkably sensible about the subject and it's partly due to his connections with South Africa. His father was assistant Private Secretary to Lord Milner, who was the British High Commissioner in South Africa after the Boer War. He married Viola, the daughter of Charles Leonard. Leonard was interesting character; he was an American who was deeply involved in the failed Jameson Raid in the Transvaal in 1895. His role was in the purchase and supply of weapons for the Raid. He operated out of Cape Town, was never put on trial, but was implicated in all the enquiries held [into the Raid]. HE with his grandfather's Cape connections had visited South Africa and had made a number of friends including Sir de Villiers Graaff, who is now the Leader of the Opposition. They had corresponded and HE's line was very much the political position of Sir de Villiers. It's difficult to summarise it briefly, but he explained that SA had a very difficult racial mix and that a policy of slow integration was far preferable to the policy of separation and the difficulties that apartheid was having on the international community. The British administration of her African colonies was based on separation rather than integration.

WE DEPART FROM AUCKLAND.

Extract of letter dated 31st March 1960.

I am sorry there have been a few days since I wrote but we have been very busy packing up in Auckland and saying goodbye to locals. It's been a very intense few weeks since the beginning of February. We had two visits recently: Lord Mountbatten was here on a high-pressure visit. You may know he is Chief of the Defence Staff in London and is doing a world tour seeing all the Commonwealth defence arrangements. I think HE was rather nervous about the visit; defence and military matters are rather outside his orbit. An interesting programme was arranged and Murray was detailed to look after him; he was on his best behaviour. In fact he was a very easy guest and appreciated all that was laid on for him. The other high-powered visitor was the Governor of the Bank of England, Lord Cobbold.

One of the problems about Auckland is that everybody seems to be squabbling with each other and they all want to trot along to HE and get him on their side. And when they are not squabbling with each other, they are squabbling with their Wellington colleagues. The St John's Ambulance organisation is rent apart. I don't fully understand the problem but Auckland raises the money and Wellington with the head branch, thinks they should dictate how it is spent. Auckland doesn't see it that way! As HE holds an honorary position as head of the organisation he is drawn into the dispute. Again, I am not sure of the details but the Boy Scouts are equally in a state of conflict. I don't think it is so much over money as over personalities and allegations of an unsuitable nature.

OFF PAINTING IN THE SOUTH ISLAND.

Extract of letter dated 8th April 1960.

The last week has been devoted to getting the Cobhams off on their leave, and packing up the house. The Cobhams left for England this afternoon. They are not expected back until the middle of June. Murray and I have decided to split the time; I am having the first four weeks away and Murray the second with a few days overlap. When everybody is away there is not much to do except answer the telephone and forward letters and just be a presence, making certain the lights are turned off in the evening and, should there be a drama, try to react…the Military Secretary, Jock Harrison, lives in a house down the drive so if anything goes wrong he can be contacted. I never mind being here on my own as I get quite a lot of painting done and I can amuse myself without difficulty. I am not sure Murray enjoys being here on his own half as much as I do……

Some time ago I was talking about my plans to go and paint in the Queenstown area to one of the honorary ADCs, Neville Hutchinson. He said his girl friend's parents lived near Queenstown and they had a batch in their garden and he was sure they wouldn't mind if I went and stayed. I think it was a small wooden hut. Anyway, Neville contacted Mrs Preston and she agreed I could use their batch. I am catching the South Island ferry tomorrow and motoring down. I have already done that road a few months ago. I am very excited as I am told all the autumn colours are at their best. The poplars have turned gold and the white snow-capped mountains behind, clear blue skies and reflections in the lakes make a wonderful scene. I can hardly think of anything more stimulating.

PAINTING IN CENTRAL OTAGO, NEAR QUEENSTOWN.

Extract of letter dated 14th April 1960.

So far everything has gone according to plan. I drove down from Lyttleton passing all the wonderful South Island lakes, which are breath taking. Arrived at the Preston batch before nightfall. The batch is very simple wooden hut but adequate; there are three rooms; two are small bedrooms and a third is a miniature kitchen, and a loo and a shower. If there is a problem, it is very cold at night so one has to sleep with a lot of clothes on. Mrs Preston asks me to join her most evenings and has been very hospitable; her husband is a lawyer in Invercargil and only appears occasionally and I have not yet met him. The batch is about two miles out of Queenstown and is ideally suited for all I want to do.

I spent the first two days driving round and getting orientated and doing a bit of exploring. I found the most exciting place was along the Skipper Road. I have to explain it is a highly dramatic place where the old gold rush miners worked along the Shotover River. The road clings to the cliffs for about six miles and leads to a graveyard where many of the miners were buried. The road is about a car's width with a sheer cliff rising hundreds of feet on one side and dropping down to the river on the other. It's not a place for the faint hearted! I explored the countryside round Lake Hayes which is fantastic at this time of year, and not far away Arrowtown, another old gold rush town. I then thought I would start painting at Lake Hayes, as I feared the wonderful colours would go.

It is simply wonderful having absolutely no other commitments all day, all the week, except to paint and totally immerse one's thoughts in trying to achieve some results and push one's humble art to the limit, with no worries, no time limit and no feeling that I was neglecting something else. I was packing up two evenings ago when a car stopped and a middle aged man got out and asked me about what I was doing…I explained I was painting and had a couple of weeks in this part of the world and we started talking. He said his name was Douglas Badcock and he was a professional artist and lived locally. After some minutes he said would I like to join him as he went out painting most days and he knew the countryside like the palm of his hand? What could be more wonderful than have this opportunity of painting with an experienced local artist?

I was at his house at eight o'clock yesterday and again this morning and we went off in his landrover. I could tell you so many things but suffice to say I am absolutely thrilled by the chance of painting with him.

PAINTING WITH DOUGLAS BADCOCK IN CENTRAL OTAGO.

Extract of letter 18th April 1960.

It is one of the most exciting things that could ever have happened to me – to find an artist whom I admire and to have the chance of painting with him. He knew exactly where to go to get the best view or the best composition. It would have taken me half a life time to have discovered these places…It is also wonderful that we paint at much the same speed…after two hours, both of us have more or less finished and we have a 'smoke O', a cup of tea, (or call it a NAFFI break). We then have a discussion about the subject and move on to another spot quite near… He is full of sensible advice. He sees me crouched over my stool… "No" he says "You want to stand up and paint, get into a rhythm and paint as you play tennis, you will get movement in your painting, your work will be much more spontaneous ..…" He was right. I now stand up and paint.

We were painting above a gorge near Queenstown yesterday. It was a fantastic place where the rocks were a mass of different colours and there was a rainbow formed from the spray of the waterfall. I made a complete mess of it. It was highly confusing and somehow even with all the excitement the subject generated I totally failed. At our 'smoke O' Douglas looked at my palate and said "Good grief, how many colours are you using?" I think I had about twelve … "No, no, you only need three. One red, one blue, and one yellow and a white and a black. Simplify everything…then all your browns and greens will be in harmony…try it." I did and it works wonderfully well. I then tried a second attempt at the gorge and I was pleased with the results.

Douglas invited me to supper last night and showed me some of his work. I am most impressed. He has a small gallery on the road near the town to sell most of his work from the gallery. His work varies from quite small studies to huge landscapes that would be suitable for public buildings…His wife mans the gallery while he goes out painting. It is an almost perfect existence!

Reflecting on his remarks nearly fifty years later, I still regard the experience I had painting with Douglas Badcock as one of the turning points in my life. Up to that moment I was quite content to soldier on and take what the Army offered and do my best, but I knew from my recent experience that painting was my passion and that somehow I must try and fit my life round my desire to paint. I was planning to get married and the financial issues and restraints would dominate my life for a long time to come. I also felt, having painted with Douglas, that I had the ability to make it as a professional artist.

Section B - ADC to the Governor General, New Zealand 1959/1960

I RETURN TO WELLINGTON.

Extract of letter dated 30th April 1960

I got back to Government House last night. I was very sad to leave Douglas Badcock and Queenstown. I think I have twelve good paintings and about four that I might be able to pull together. I long to return but I don't see that I will have the chance again, as once HE returns next month, we have a very full programme in July and August and in September, I am on my way to you …

I was quite amused by an incident last weekend. As I have explained, I was staying in the batch belonging to the Prestons. They couldn't have been kinder and I appreciated their hospitality. Last weekend Neville Hutchinson came down from Wellington to ask old Mr Preston if he could marry his daughter, Jane. Now old Mr Preston only appears occasionally and got completely mixed up. Neville spent the weekend helping Mr Preston saw-up wood and do a mass of menial tasks and making himself useful in every way, but every time he started on the subject of wanting to marry Jane, Old Mr Preston said "You know that joker in the cottage, he's after her too!" Neville came to me and said "For God's sake put the old man right, that I am the one who wants to marry Jane, and not yourself…" Well, it wasn't quite that easy. When we had supper together that evening Mr Preston wasn't having it that I wasn't the suitor… "You have been here long enough to get to know the family Philip. Margaret says you're a good bloke and that's what I like!" Poor old Neville was climbing up the wall and getting nowhere with the old man…I did my best and I think in the end Mrs Preston had to put her husband right.

It was good to see Murray again; he had survived the last month and was remarkably cheerful. He said it was a bit like being stranded on a desert island being on his own here for nearly a month in an utterly deserted Government House. He is due to go off latter this week. I think he has friends in Hawke Bay.

HOUSE SITTING AT GOVERNMENT HOUSE AND PAINTING.

Extract of letter dated 12th May 1960.

Murray left last Thursday and I am now on my own for more than three weeks…Having been on my own in Central Otago for three weeks, except for my painting with Douglas and the occasional supper with the Prestons, I am quite happy on my own. I have got a good routine which keeps me sane. After breakfast I meet with the Sergeant Major (he is a sort of rather grand messenger and security man). He delivers the mail and takes away any mail that needs posting. Some mornings Dave Fouhy or his assistant, John Purvis, appear. I go round to their office and chat them up, sometimes Kitty Wood the Secretary, looks in and does some work…I hang around the offices till about midday and if the weather is reasonable, I collect my sandwiches from the kitchen and go off painting. I try to be back by about five, I have supper at six, a time that suits the kitchen staff. I check the house is closed down and I read till about nine and turn in. I have covered great distances and found some sensational places to paint …I think my work is more advanced as a result of painting with Douglas, and I am very excited about all I am doing.

Extract of letter dated 19th May 1960.

My routine has continued…. I feel rather foolish telling you the same story again and again. We have had some rather nasty weather and winter is evidently here. It has prevented me going out and doing much… The Williston Galleries have given me a date for an exhibition, 30th August to 9th September. I am very pleased as it gives me a target to work for. It is the way of things that some of my earlier work, which I was quite pleased with at the time, is a long way behind my last batch of paintings, so I expect I will paint over them. I have also got a problem of space as the only place I can keep my work is in my bedroom. I can put the odd painting in the office when its dry, but that's not very popular as some weeks ago Murray was just about to go out, looking very smart in his 'whites', and somehow he managed to get paint all over his uniform…and he had to change at the last minute; it was not very popular!

There is a gap in my letters from the middle of May 1960...I have explained the circumstances.

MY ILLNESS AND DEPARTURE FROM NEW ZEALAND.

Soon after I returned to Government House, I became ill with acute stomach pains. After a while there was nothing for it but to go into Wellington Hospital. I think the doctors were puzzled to know what was wrong, and they thought I was suffering from adhesions. They operated and found nothing wrong. It would not be too dramatic to say I was very ill when one day Yvonne Cumming Bruce came to see me. She was the wife of the British High Commissioner and only recently arrived in New Zealand. I had got to know her; she was an artist and a stepsister to my predecessor, Blair Stewart-Wilson. As I lay in bed feeling dreadful, she asked me what was wrong and I explained that the doctors were still struggling to find out. What I did not know was that she was an experienced herbalist. She looked at my hands and said, "You have got lead poisoning – all the lines on your hands are yellow. You have got yellow on your eye lids." She told the doctors I was suffering from lead poisoning. They then conducted a series of tests, which confirmed Yvonne's diagnosis. I was in hospital for about two weeks but I dread to think what my fate might have been had it not been for Yvonne's intervention.

The antidote for lead poisoning is calcium. The lead never leaves one's system; it lodges in the marrow of one's bones and remains there for a very long time. To bring pain relief it is necessary to adjust the chemical balance, which is achieved by a substantial intake of calcium. Several times over the next ten years these acute pains have returned and by drinking a large quantity of milk I was able to control it.

There was a major concern as to how I had developed lead poisoning. It was almost unheard of and certainly the medical profession hadn't experienced it in Wellington. Could I have developed it as a result of living in Government House, or possibly, from my stay in the Preston batch in Queenstown? Who else might be affected? There was an official inquiry, which concluded that I had developed the poison from using flake white, a pigment, which is almost neat lead, during my painting. It had often been said that I had sucked my brushes, which was not true, but I think what had happened was that over a long period I had built up a dangerous level of lead while I was painting. Over the last nine months I had many picnic lunches and gradually a small amount of paint on my hands must have been transferred to the sandwiches. I must have absorbed enough lead to cause the effects that nearly killed me.

When I got back to Government House, I was in a weak state and to get my strength back, it was decided that I should go and stay with Julie Wilding's family in the South Island at their lovely property Te Mania on the Cheviot Flats. They were extremely kind to me and it was a lovely part of the world. Their next-door neighbour was Charles Upham who is one of very few people who was ever awarded a bar to his Victoria Cross. I had the honour of getting to know him and I was struck by his quiet modesty; his life was that of a simple sheep farmer. He hated the publicity and fame his award had brought him; he just wanted to be left alone with his family and sheep.

I returned to Government House, completely revived and fit, a few days before HE and Lady C returned in the middle of June. We quickly got back into the routine of dinner parties and visits. The Opening of Parliament at the end of the month. July and August passed quickly. I had my painting exhibition at the Williston Galleries from the 30th August till 9th September. I asked Yvonne Cumming Bruce to open it and it was my farewell party. As so often happens, it's very difficult to gauge its success but my paintings sold well. I had a good write up in the press and there were a number of complimentary and kind remarks. I felt it was a very fitting and suitable way to end my time in New Zealand as I could show people how I had seen the wonderful landscape of the country. I also felt I had achieved something beyond being an ordinary ADC.

I left Government House feeling deeply sad that I had had to depart in a hurry. For thirteen months everybody at Government House had been like my family and it was a painful wrench leaving; I never had a proper chance to say goodbye to a great many kind friends in Wellington. I had grown to love New Zealand and admire the people. I had fallen in love with the landscape; so much of the New Zealand relaxed way of life appealed to me.

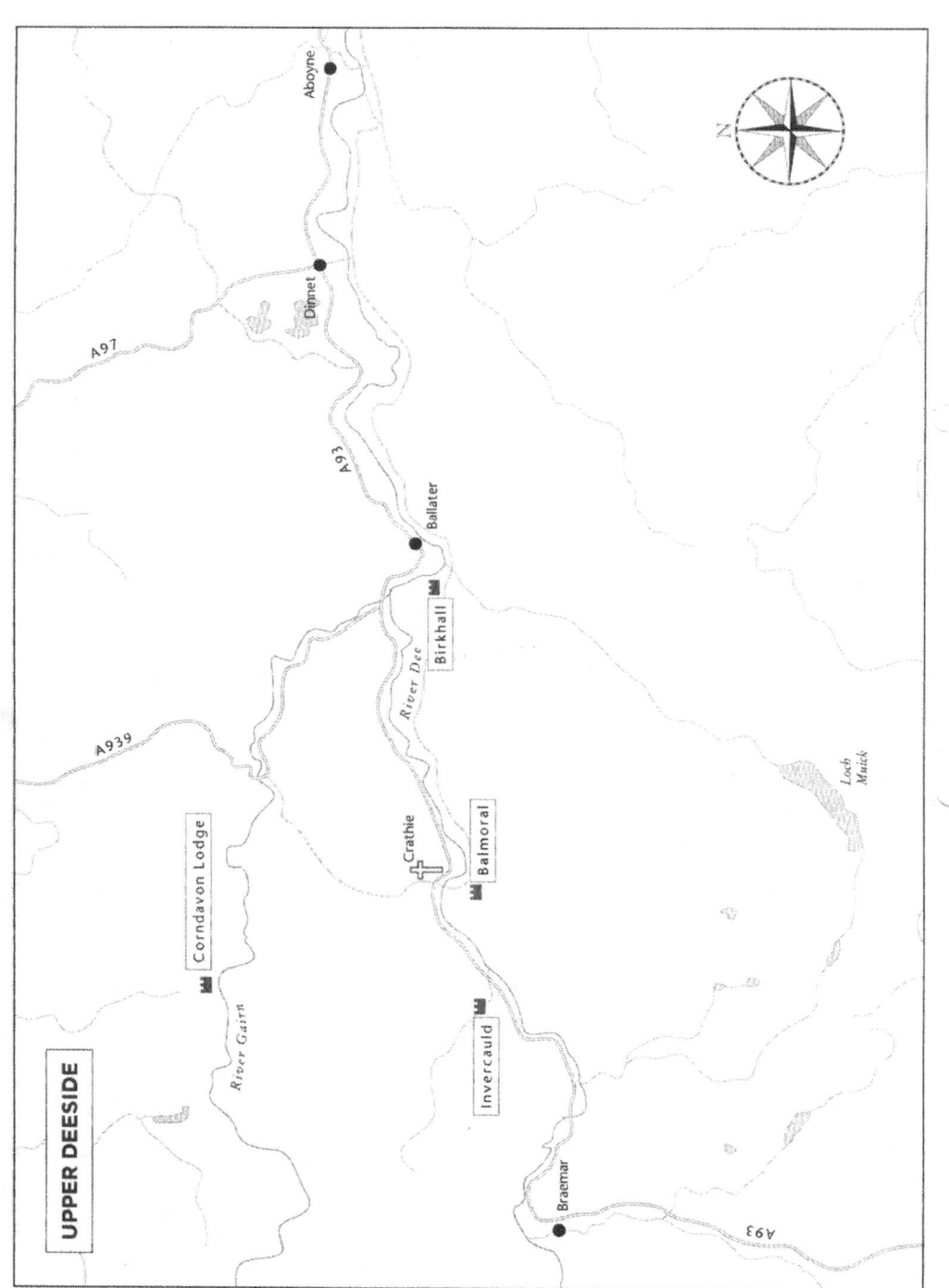

Section C

Queen's Guard, Balmoral

Along with other ceremonial guards provided for Her Majesty The Queen, a detachment of infantry soldiers is normally based at Ballater when she travels to Balmoral Castle on Deeside for her summer holiday. This duty is more often than not performed by a Scottish Infantry battalion based in Edinburgh but in 1967, not long after the 1st Battalion's return from the Far East and when stationed at Redford Barracks in the city, the Scots Guards were selected to undertake the duty.

In 1967 Philip Erskine commanded the detachment deployed from Edinburgh, which was stationed in the local Ballater barracks for the months of August, September and early October.

Apart from two guards of honour to mark the Queen's arrival and departure from Balmoral, there were few military duties for those involved although a number of other regular commitments fell to the Guard. Some of these involved being at close quarters with the Royal Family and were generally much enjoyed.

The following selection of letters were written by Philip to his mother in 1967. They reflect both the military and social aspects of the two month deployment. They have been edited in order to eliminate any matters of a personal nature concerning the Royal family, any unnecessary repetition and to remove material sensitive to the Erskine family or not approved by them. Otherwise they are much as Philip wrote them.

1st Battalion Scots Guards, Ballater
4th August 1967

Many thanks for your letter. We arrived up here on Tuesday and got settled into our cottage and then Fiona went back to collect Nanny yesterday, Thursday, and is returning today. The cottage is rather primitive and strangely decorated with odd furniture. However, this part of the world is perfect…

Wednesday I went and saw some of the locals. The minister at Crathie, is a delightful person who told us the form at church…..

Have been round to see some of the local lairds and it is really most amusing. I went to see Captain Sir Alwyne (Ian) Farquharson of Invercauld. Invercauld is a huge castle, some of it Victorian, but much of it very ancient. He has a second castle – Braemar Castle – on the other side of the Dee which was Lord Mar's and in fact he raised his standard for the 1715 rebellion there. After his defeat the Farquharsons obtained most of his land and the castle and a great deal of the local land was Erskine.

There are still a large number of people I have to go and see and this is going to take up much of my time. I have got 4 very pleasant officers; Kim Fraser, one of Lovat's sons; Anthony Forbes, a local; David Drummond Moray, his parents live at Abercairney in Perthshire; Andrew Parsons and his wife are very pleasant so it is quite an amusing party……

Section C - Queen's Guard, Balmoral

Tornasheen, Ballater, Aberdeenshire, Ballater 541
5th August 1967

Please note my telephone number. A million thanks for your very long letter…

Fiona arrived in one piece from Edinburgh loaded up to the eye balls with all Nanny's stuff and Edward; everything was brought (!) and as a result she can hardly move in her room. I told her one suitcase – 4 came! However, she has settled in and seems quite happy.

Last night I took Fiona to have a drink at Crathie Manse. The minister is a delightful person – very nice wife and both were very sweet to Fiona and gave her a briefing for what the form is for the 'excitements' after the Queen arrives. There is quite a lot of detail to absorb. We get asked to both of the Ghillies' Balls and to dine. The Minister says he has a large job during the Queen's visit of two months as nearly every Sunday there is a visiting preacher who always by tradition stays at Balmoral and he has to brief them on all aspects of their stay.

Tornasheen
11th August 1967

The Queen arrives here on Monday 14th and we provide a Guard of Honour at Balmoral Gates to meet her. It is quite short and quick and under normal circumstances nothing of much note. However, because it is the first time the Brigade of Guards has done the Guard and because we are not wearing bearskins, and, instead of tunics the officers are wearing frockcoats, it is all creating Press interest. The Queen has expressed the wish that bearskins should not be worn – too formal for Balmoral is the reason given. Anyway, lots of silly telephone calls all day. The other game the press are trying to play is to get someone fairly senior in the Highland Brigade to make some adverse comment about our doing it. So far they haven't had any joy on that one. But I was on Scottish BBC TV this evening practising the Guard. I didn't see it but several people have rung me up!

Invitations to dine and to shoot were heaped upon Philip throughout his time at Ballater. On 12th he was invited to shoot with a former Scots Guardsman, Colonel Crabbe, whose son had recently also served in the Regiment.

You would be quite amused. By tradition a small present every year is given by the officers of the Guard to Princess Anne for her birthday. It is not very easy to know what to get. It mustn't be too expensive so I went and had a look round an old antique shop, and, after a long rummage, I found a pair of attractive cut glass scent bottles, about 8" high, something for her dressing table. Cost 35/- the pair so for the five officers 7/- each. I don't think one could get better value for money….. If it had been later I would have given her a picture but I haven't yet had a chance to do any painting.

All the sergeants have been doing highland dancing classes, getting practice for the Ghillies' balls which are 31st August and 21st September.

The general opinion up here is that the grouse are very poor. There was a lot of very cold weather in May and most of the nests were destroyed. However, on Tuesday I had a practice for the beaters and we walked in an extended line about 3 miles up the glen and down again and there were quite a number of old birds but almost no young ones. [*During its time on Deeside the Guard would help out on shooting days on the Balmoral moors by beating. All ranks participated with one of the officers 'in command' of the line.*]

I never take my kilt off. One man came up to me and said "I see you have the Erskine tartan on. I have one myself." I enquired why so and he said "Oh, well I needed one for the Highland Games so I fancied this one in a shop in Aberdeen."

[*It is reported*] that everyone in Aberdeenshire is always very interested in the Guard. The word has gone round that 'Mrs Erskine is very pretty and Mrs Parsons (my second in command's wife) wears mini skirts. Minis are much frowned on up here, I assume!' [*NB. The veracity of this report has not been substantiated!*].

Ballater
15th August 1967

Yesterday I think went quite well. The Queen arrived a little late, but the rain had stopped and she inspected us in a summer hat and coat. We all went up for a drink in the evening, including Fiona. We were met by Prince Andrew who showed us in. The Queen talked to us for about an hour and a quarter…..

Ballater
19th August 1967

This week has been just non-stop. I have hardly had a moment to think about anything other than the activity in hand.

Three days this week I have been shooting, walking up grouse across the moor. The first day, Wednesday, was at Invercauld with Captain Sir Alwyne Farquharson of Invercauld. We shot 40 brace, just three guns – he and I with an American. The American was killing every time a bird got up: there were cries of "there goes another cotton tail" or "Gee, I've run out of shells" (meaning 'he hadn't got a cartridge up the breach'). Alwyne Farquharson gets $1,700 a week for a couple to stay and be treated as a guest - the whole works and full Highland hospitality is laid on by a real chief. This includes being dined in the ancestral home with the table a mass of heather, tartan table mats, tartan everything; being taken to Crathie Church; as much grouse shooting and fishing as the guest can do. In fact he lays on a cross between a safari and the Duke of Bedford's treatment at Woburn. He has 2 or 3 couples a year and on this he keeps Invercauld going – all 240,000 acres of nothing.

We start providing beaters for driving at Balmoral from next Tuesday and then it is 4 or 5 days a week for the guardsmen who are divided into two teams taking it in turns……

I have just returned from delivering Princess Anne's present at the castle and nearly ran over Prince Andrew and Lord Linley who were racing each other on their tricycles on the drive. Two typical naughty boys!

1st Battalion Scots Guards
21st August 1967

Yesterday at Crathie Church it was quite amusing. The Guard march to church with the officers and we sit opposite the Queen's pew. Very hard not to stare. Well, we thought Nanny would enjoy the scene although with Edward she couldn't come into the church. Outside were 40 press men and a crowd of 6,000. They all thought Nanny was one of the Royal nannies; Nanny remained silent and the mystery deepened! She was jostled here and there……the 40 press men had nothing to do for an hour while the Queen was in church, their attention focused on Edward and Nanny! Then afterwards they wanted to picture her with the Minister. She never said who she was or who Edward belonged to; it would have spoilt the effect! She heard comments from the crowd: "All Royal babies are taught to sit so upright" and "You can see how beautifully kept the baby is, the gloves he is wearing". In another letter dated 27th August Philip adds that one reporter asked if Edward was a Viscount!

Nanny out for a walk in Ballater!

Tornasheen
3rd September 1967

The Ghillies' Ball was highly amusing; it was a cross between a village dance with all the Balmoral staff including the keepers, stalkers, housemaids and the soldiers, and a small private dance with the Balmoral and Birkhall house parties and a few invited guests: the local minister, the factor and doctor plus the Household staff and the officers of the Guard. At 9.30pm we all went to Balmoral and collected in the drawing room and met everyone. When the word was given we went and shook hands with the Queen and made our way down to the Ballroom. It was like a page out of Lady Longford's book, the Life of Queen Victoria.

There were about 25 guardsmen invited, all in red tunics, and with pipers and the kilted figures the effect was most colourful. Very shortly after we got there the Queen came down the stairs from the Minstrels' Gallery and the Ball started. We started by doing an eightsome reel, the four officers of the Guard just next to the Queen's set. This was followed by a Paul Jones and so on, another reel and a waltz……. The Queen asked me to get her two Sergeants to do the Dashing White Sergeant with. Several of the guardsmen danced with members of the Royal party. The Queen left about midnight and we all followed her to the drawing room. The party went on till about 2 am.

[*Philip records that the next week or so included appearances at both the Aboyne and Braemar Games*]. Not for 12 years have I danced so much, been to so many parties, eaten so much, drunk so much, enjoyed life so much and indeed felt so exhausted! Every party is so far away and involves such driving which is the only part I don't much enjoy.

1st Battalion Scots Guards
7th September 1967

Wednesday – yesterday – was the Aboyne Games. They are a miniature edition of Braemar and much more fun. Everyone knows everybody. I lunched with the Chief and in its own way it was very colourful. All the family flags were out all round the field. Forbes of this and that and Gordons of this and that dominate the flags. Quite a few for Glen Tanar, and Cowdray and Astor all had their flags up. There was a procession of the Chiefs led by the Moderator [*Church of Scotland*] and Lord Lyon [*Lord Lyon King of Arms, responsible for the control of hereditary in Scotland*] and the Chiefs with their eagles' feathers and Inverness capes. The games themselves were far from dull. The dancing was very interesting and colourful and I could watch that all day. Children hardly older than Rupert danced most beautifully. There was the caber, a brand new one which no one could toss – a huge tree trunk over 20 ft – and when all the contestants had failed, they produced an old one! Then there was a drama when the hammer came off its handle and, by good luck, hurt no one.

Then there was a tug of war. I am afraid the Guard was rather easily beaten by the US Marines team, all men of 20 stone. There's no weight limit. So indeed were the local farmers' team, in their case it was not due to weight but alcohol! I gather the whiff of whisky was enough to almost intoxicate their opponents. We did win a few events; the local piping was one. We had all 5 places but only 5 contestants took part – all else withdrew.

It is all quite an experience with wizened old boys walking round clutching their crooks, draped in Inverness capes and the very smartest have eagles' feathers in their bonnets. The women wear as much tartan as possible, except some wear as little as possible! One girl who acted as a host – the daughter of the Marquess of Huntley -- wore a mini kilt and shawl.

Section C - Queen's Guard, Balmoral

Tornasheen
10th September 1967

…………the previous day was the Braemar Games. They are so different to the Aboyne Games. Braemar is 100% commercial – huge stands packed to capacity. We had tickets just next to the Royal Box but we had to stay put and couldn't walk about. The Scots Guards Pipe Band were the winners of the Pipe Band contest against about 12 other top level bands. The Queen was delighted…..

Tornasheen, Ballater
20th September 1967

I had a lovely day shooting at Balmoral today. The form is that one goes to the Gun Room with one's gun and cartridges at 9.10 and hands them to the keeper. One's gun is placed in a rack on the side of a landrover and one's cartridges are placed in a large shallow wooden box fixed to the bonnet of the same landrover. One then goes to the Equerry room where one is told who the other guns are and kicks about for 15 minutes until one goes along to the front hall where one is introduced to the other guns. Today as the Queen was launching the new Queen Elizabeth II [*on the river Clyde*], Prince Philip went with her and Prince Charles was acting as the host.

Anyway we all bundled into a very smart long wheel based landrover and off to the moor. It couldn't have been a more unpromising day – the glass was low; NE wind; low cloud so it was decided to do some of the very low strips along the Gairn river. We had 4 drives in the morning and 2 in the afternoon.

We had lunch beside the burn and, as the Queen was away, she had asked the Queen Mother to act as host....Half way through lunch the Queen Mother said "Major Erskine, I have been meaning to ask you for several days if you would paint me a picture........" "Yes, Mam, I would be very honoured". "Well it's rather more than a picture, it's a whole wall", her eyes twinkling, "Oh, please try if you have time. It's on the wall of my shooting lodge lunch place at Corndavon". Anyway I said I would. We discussed it a little and she wants something to break up the bareness of the walls. So that is my new job!! [*Corndavon Lodge is on the Invercauld Estate further up the Gairn river from where they were picnic-ing*].

Queen's Guard, Ballater
22nd September 1967

Last night was the second Ghillies' Ball. Very nearly the same as last time. We dined with the Minister, Mr and Mrs Budge, at the Manse, a delightful house beside the Dee. One rather interesting thing Mrs Budge showed me. Queen Victoria ordered 2 windows which overlooked the graveyard – John Brown's grave is there – to be blocked up and a third window had rough glazing in it in order no one should gaze at her when she visited John Brown's grave.

Mr Budge has asked me to read the lesson the last Sunday. Prince Philip reads the other lesson.

The Royal party was rather smaller than last time. The Queen Mother had a very small party.......The first dance at the Ghillies' Ball was an eightsome and we had an all Guard set. Then the Paul Jones, then a Dashing White Sergeant; again the Queen asked me like last time if I could get 2 sergeants for her which I did. There were in all 10 dances; the only one I couldn't do properly was the Scottish Country Waltz.

Tornasheen
29th September 1967

I had a lovely day stalking yesterday at Invercauld. It was a perfectly glorious day and the stalker took me right up on the high ground. Deer everywhere in herds of 50 at least. One herd of nearly 200 but they move on quickly if disturbed and the large herds are very difficult to get close enough to stalk and shoot. Late in the evening I shot a stag and this involved a considerable walk back to get the ponyman with his pony to take the dead beast down the hill, and then back to the landrover and it was dark by the time we got back to the vehicle. The beauty of the hills is staggering and by far the best part of it all.

Tonight a small dinner in the Mess with Prince Philip and several local ex-Brigade of Guards. Lord Forbes, ex-Grenadier; Colonel Crabbe who was in the regiment; John Gibb also was in the regiment and an old boy Burges Lumsden who lives at Pitcaple Castle, ex Coldstream. I asked General Geordie Gordon Lennox but he had someone staying.

Did I tell you the story of the guardsman at the Ghillies' Ball? During the first Paul Jones he got the Queen Mother; the next time he got the Queen. The Queen Mother as she passed the guardsman said out of the corner of her mouth to him 'Snob….!' Rather a sweet story.

Tornasheen
1st October 1967

[*In a letter of the previous day Philip wrote about his sister, Polly, having had a motor accident*]. I have been thinking about Polly's motor accident. I think she is very lucky not to be worse. It always seems that the worst motor accidents in London always happen after midnight.

I had a motor accident on my hands this morning. They always go in twos. One of my three tonners carrying 20 guardsmen beaters out to the moor was hit full on by a cattle truck on a very narrow road. The army vehicle was able to brake to a stand but nevertheless the impact was considerable. All the men in the back of the vehicle were thrown forward; 4 were hurt: 2 were taken to Aberdeen Hospital. One had a fractured pelvis, the other only badly concussed. The lucky thing was that the accident happened on part of the road which had 30 ft vertical drop and the police reckon, if our driver had had to swerve, he would have skidded off the road and I dread to think the loss of life involved. Anyway I had all the lines buzzing: the Press; the Queen; Highland District; the Battalion all wanting to know. I went out at lunchtime and told Prince Philip the exact details as I had them from the hospital.

I must tell you the story of Guardsman Coventry, how he hadn't ever fished before and with a sergeant he went out to the Gairn (a tributary of the Dee which the Queen allows the Guard to fish). His second cast ever he hooked a large fish. The Gairn is a very small stream, he had a 7lb fish on his line and in due course landed it. Well, the question was what was the fish; it was dark brown same as a trout but its tail was that of a salmon. The expert verdict was that it is very rare hybrid, a cross between a salmon and a trout. The outcome is that all fish, except trout, have to be sent up to the Queen. Poor Coventry had lost his fish and it had been sent to an experimental fish farm research station for tests! The poor man was almost in tears.

Tornasheen
5th October 1967

I was asked to stalk at Balmoral yesterday so I went up to the Castle at 9 equipped with stick, field glasses and correct cap, looking like a Punch figure. The form is you go to the Equerry's room where you get your instructions from the Equerry, Lord Plunkett. I was to go to Spital or Bachnagain, both areas of high ground on which nothing exists except the odd deer. I hadn't the faintest idea which would offer the most likely chance of shooting a deer, but I had 2 guardsmen who live in a bothy beside Loch Muick and each day they go up with their two ponies to a shelter 2,500 feet up on the Bachnagain, a high plateau above Loch Muick and I thought it would be fun to see them.......... there was a general discussion on the prospects with the Head Keeper, ghillies and the others who were going out......

Anyway we were given our picnic lunch which included a small flask of whisky and some delicious eats, introduced to the young ghillie who was to take me out and then off we set. I had 2 practice shots at a steel target stag in the drive to feel the rifle I was lent by Balmoral. The drive out was 22 miles, a hell of a drive right across the property almost to the furthest point. The last five miles was quite hair raising. The track which is only the width of a landrover climbs 2,000 ft right up sheer above Loch Muick. It was blowing a hurricane with torrential rain; visibility wasn't very good and always one had a sheer cliff on one side. The track was almost a river and the young boy I was driving in my landrover was petrified! At one point a burn flowing over the cliff was being blown back up the hill and it looked like smoke rising! When we got up to the top it was sleet and snow. The landscape was the bleakest imaginable.

There was a small stone hut with 2 ponies inside; my two guardsmen perfectly happy and it looked like the hut in the film 'Scott of the Antarctic'. The old wizened stalker, Henderson, said "It's nay the day for stalking" and we waited for an hour or so before returning. It was almost worse going down the hill as the wind was behind us; can you think of anything more unpleasant going down a steep track with a precipice on one side and the track almost a river and slippery as hell plus a visibility of 10yds!

However, we managed it all and I had my picnic lunch by the edge of Loch Muick in peace and quiet, looking back up the hill, still encased in the storm, and looking across the loch to the Gasult where Queen Victoria had built a house and spent many days of her widowhood in almost complete isolation. The scene couldn't have changed one fraction from the many she must have seen. There is no sign of human activity apart from the one small house…

We have our final Guard of Honour on Sunday. The Queen inspects us outside the Castle and we march past her on the way to church. There are two more beating days and then the Guard leaves on Thursday 12th after lunch, the Queen before lunch. I am staying on to do the mural [at Corndavon].

Last night we had an all ranks dance. They are absolute hell, however one has to have them. In order to draw the girls, one young officer advertised the item 'Beauty contest. Miss Royal Guard 1967'. What happened was that about six very drunken soldiers chose a large 'bag' and I was invited to crown her! I was damned if I was going to kiss her….she kissed me! Well, all went quite well, we made some money and the guardsmen enjoyed themselves.

Queen's Guard
7th October 1967

We have been slightly involved in the Field Trials at Balmoral, providing a number of guardsmen to do jobs.

We had a Sergeants' Mess party last night. They asked all the keepers, stalkers and ghillies from Balmoral.

Patrick Plunket, the Equerry, rang late last night and said "Would there be any officers who would like to stalk tomorrow?" I said I could detail one but everyone was committed. Patrick rang back and said Prince Philip would like the two Warrant Officers to go out. They (D/Sgt Armitage and CSM Meade) were delighted.

In the Queens Guard game book we have beaten the Grouse total, a general total up to 1933 and only 300 behind with a week to go. We lie second behind 1922 but there is no hope of beating this, a 1,000 ahead of us. We have shot 5,000 grouse. 1922 was the best year ever. The records in the book go back to 1899. Rather a fascinating book.

Tornasheen
10th October 1967

The last three days have been so busy. On Sunday we paraded at Balmoral at 1045 providing a Guard of Honour just outside the front door. The Queen inspected us and then we marched past her, and then marched to Church. We then had our final, farewell, church service. I read the 1st lesson – Isaiah Chapter 55 to the end of the chapter. Prince Philip the second lesson. Fiona made me practice reading and I think it went off quite well.

Then yesterday just as I was off shooting, Patrick Plunket rang at 9am and said the Queen had asked us to dine…. [*During dinner there was some amused discussion of an earlier incident involving what was described ….*] as the 'Frankenstein' figure of a guardsman who looked after one of the ponies who had appeared during a picnic. Apparently he had taken his pony to water it, straight through the Royal Picnic, knocking everything for six, heavy pony hooves running over all the Royal rugs. Everyone seemed very amused about the incident. [*The pony handler was L/Cpl Brizzle of the Scots Guards*].

This evening the Queen and Prince Philip and the Queen Mother all came to the barracks. I took them first to the Sergeants Mess and then to the Officers Mess. They all said how much they enjoyed having the Scots Guards up here. The Queen said several times "Thank you for all you have done" and what a good Guard it had been. They stayed for about 1 ¼ hours and it was lovely to have them in our small Mess.

Tornasheen
14th October 1967

The Queen left Balmoral on Thursday 12th at 1100. Fiona and I with 3 officers went to the gates to wave her good-bye.

[*Philip was asked to shoot at Dinnet with Lady Barclay Harvey and to take Fiona with him*].

It was a lovely sunny but cold day. We shot about 60 pheasants and 6 brace of partridges and grouse. Fiona brought Twinkie out. Don't laugh – Twinkie has an excellent nose and very good eyesight. She notices where the birds fall and she goes and sits beside them. In fact far from being a little fool she was extremely quick. I had 5 down in a drive and she had all of them in quite deep heather which I wouldn't ever have found. I thought much better than the Labradors; they go off at a great pace, over running the spot. KoKo is gun shy and remains in the car shaking!

I have offered 2 spare beds in my cottage for 2 officers of the battalion to stalk. The estate want more stags shot. They are very much behind their quota. The two young men here at present are Michael Nurton and Mark Tennant.

The Station Hotel, Perth
14th October 1967

[*Philip received the following letter from Martin Charteris*].

On her departure from Balmoral The Queen commanded me to write to you to let you know how satisfied she has been with the conduct of the guard this year. Her Majesty would be grateful if you would convey to all ranks under your command an expression of her thanks and appreciation for the services and duties they have carried out so admirably during her visit to Deeside.

The Queen was impressed by their smartness on and off parade, and by the cheerfulness with which they carried out their tasks at Balmoral and on the hill. Her Majesty sends her best wishes to all ranks for the future.

[Sir Martin Charteris].

Postscript. *Philip completed the Corndavon mural and in September 1968 Fiona and he were invited by the Queen Mother to stay at Birkhall. During their stay they picnic-ed by the Lodge at Corndavon with its newly painted mural. Philip's work was greatly admired and seemingly enjoyed by all.*

Epilogue

Philip and I only served together once in the Scots Guards and that was in the 1st Battalion in the late 1960s. In 1969 the battalion was stationed in London and that year it was to troop its Queen's Colour on the Birthday Parade. Murray de Klee was our Commanding Officer and he was to command the parade as the Field Officer in Brigade Waiting. Philip had been selected to command No 2 Guard while I was to command the Escort to the Colour.

On the day of the parade all went well; with the end in sight the eight Guards had just completed the march past in slow time and were by then about to commence marching past The Queen in quick time. As the Escort, followed closely by No 2 Guard, reached the final forming point on the Downing Street side of Horse Guards Parade, both had to mark time, one behind the other, until ready to go forward past the saluting dais. As a result they had to bunch up in close proximity to each other, probably for less than a minute. As we all marked time at the forming point, I distinctly recall hearing Philip's voice regaling his guardsmen with shouts of 'keep going', 'not far now' and 'well done' and so on. Not only did he shout such encouragement but he turned around to face his Guard, leaving his position to move up and down the ranks, while continuing to mark time himself. Doubtless such a thing may have been done before, but as an example of spontaneous if idiosyncratic leadership, it was hard to beat and typical of Philip….and of course it had the desired effect on his guardsmen.

1969. Philip in the centre of No 2 Guard